Collyer's Library - Phone 01403 216548

XX34338

D0333212

AS/A2

Music Technology
Study Guide

Second Edition

Edexcel

Jonny Martin

R·

Rhinegold Education

239–241 Shaftesbury Avenue
London WC2H 8TF
Telephone: 020 7333 1720
Fax: 020 7333 1765

www.rhinegold.co.uk

THE COLLEGE OF
RICHARD COLLYER
LIBRARY

Music Study Guides

GCSE, AS and A2 Music Study Guides (AQA, Edexcel and OCR)
GCSE, AS and A2 Music Listening Tests (AQA, Edexcel and OCR)
GCSE Music Study Guide (WJEC)
GCSE Music Listening Tests (WJEC)
AS/A2 Music Technology Study Guide (Edexcel)
AS/A2 Music Technology Listening Tests (Edexcel)
Revision Guides for GCSE (AQA, Edexcel and OCR), AS and A2 Music (Edexcel)

Also available from Rhinegold Education

Key Stage 3 Elements
Key Stage 3 Listening Tests: Book 1 and Book 2
AS and A2 Music Harmony Workbooks
GCSE and AS Music Composition Workbooks
GCSE and AS Music Literacy Workbooks
Romanticism in Focus, Baroque Music in Focus, Film Music in Focus,
Modernism in Focus, *The Immaculate Collection* in Focus, *Who's Next* in Focus,
Batman in Focus, *Goldfinger* in Focus, Musicals in Focus,
Music Technology from Scratch

Rhinegold also publishes Choir & Organ, Classical Music, Classroom Music, Early Music Today,
International Piano, Music Teacher, MUSO, Opera Now, Piano, The Singer, Teaching Drama,
British and International Music Yearbook, British Performing Arts Yearbook, British Music Education Yearbook,
World Conservatoires, Rhinegold Dictionary of Music in Sound

Other Rhinegold Study Guides

Rhinegold also publishes resources for candidates studying Drama and Theatre Studies.

First published 2009 in Great Britain by
Rhinegold Education
239–241 Shaftesbury Avenue
London WC2H 8TF
Telephone: 020 7333 1720
Fax: 020 7333 1765
www.rhinegold.co.uk

Reprinted 2009

© Rhinegold Publishing Ltd 2009

All rights reserved. No part of this publication may be reproduced, stored in a retrieval system,
or transmitted in any form or by any means, electronic, mechanical, photocopying, recording or otherwise,
without the prior permission of Rhinegold Publishing Ltd.

This title is excluded from any licence issued by the Copyright Licensing Agency,
or other Reproduction Rights Organisation.

Rhinegold Publishing Ltd has used its best efforts in preparing this workbook. It does not assume, and hereby
disclaims, any liability to any party for loss or damage caused by errors or omissions in the Guide
whether such errors or omissions result from negligence, accident or other cause.

If you are preparing for an exam in music you should always carefully check
the current requirements of the examination, since these may change from one year to the next.

Edexcel AS/A2 Music Technology Study Guide
British Library Cataloguing in Publication Data.
A catalogue record for this book is available from the British Library.
ISBN: 978-1-906178-48-2
Printed by Headley Brothers Ltd

Author

Jonny Martin is Chair of Examiners for Edexcel GCE Music Technology and GCSE Music. He has been Head of Music in two comprehensive schools teaching across the secondary age range. He has also been a peripatetic guitar teacher, teaching electric, classical and bass guitar. Alongside his education activities, he has always maintained a performing schedule, regularly performing around the country in a number of different ensembles. He is co-author of Edexcel GCSE Music (with John Arkell) and is a music consultant for the Qualifications and Curriculum Authority. He has a passion for music education, delivering workshops and training for teachers and students across the UK.

Acknowledgments

The author would like to thank Michael Lovelock for his work on the illustrations, Chris Duffill and Mortimer Rhind-Tutt for their advice and suggestions, and Matthew Hammond and Ben Smith of Rhinegold publishing for their editorial and design work.

Edexcel's GCE in Music Technology is a challenging and exciting specification, designed to introduce you to the skills and knowledge you need to work in the music technology industry. By following the course you will develop your practical skills and your ability to listen analytically to music so that you can ensure your work meets the highest standards. You will have opportunities to express yourself musically through creative use of music technology and using the technology as a performance tool.

This book will guide you through every aspect of the course, giving you definitive advice on how to tackle each element of the practical work and how to prepare yourself for the written examinations. It gives insights into what the examiner is looking for in your work so that you can avoid common pitfalls, present your work in the best possible light and maximise your potential. It is intended to contain sufficient information to see you through your AS and A2 courses, but is not a replacement for a skilled teacher. Your level of success will depend on how much work you are willing to put into the course but, if you follow all the guidance given in these pages, you will give yourself the best possible chance of success in the qualification.

Edexcel GCE Music Technology

Structure of the course

AS		A2	
Unit 1 One sequenced perform- ance One multi-track recording One arrangement Logbook	35%	**Unit 3** One sequenced integrated performance One multi-track recording One composition Logbook	30%
Unit 2 Listening and Analysing: 1 hr 45 min examination	15%	**Unit 4** Analysing and Producing: 2 hr examination	20%

Units 1 and 2 are worth 100% of the AS level and 50% of the full GCE. Units 3 and 4 are worth 100% of the A2 level and 50% of the full GCE.

This guide will take you through each of the units in turn, explaining the requirements of each unit and how you might best go about meeting them.

Before undertaking any task for an examination it is vital to consider the following:

- What does the task entail?
- What is the examiner looking for?
- What are the rules for completing the task?
- How can I best use my time to complete the task?
- How can I make best use of the equipment available to me?

What does the task entail?

The sequencing task requires you to **listen** to an original track and to try and **recreate** the track in your sequence. There are marks available for creativity, but this is more about how you creatively solve the problems inherent in the completion of the task rather than adding any of your own creative input to the original stimulus.

> The golden rule, and something you should constantly remind yourself, is: the original audio track is the standard by which any sequence is judged. Everything you do should resemble the original audio track as closely as is humanly possible. Do not do anything to try and improve the original track; copy it, warts and all.

The skeleton score provided by Edexcel as a stimulus is a useful starting point and contains a lot of information which you can directly copy into your sequence, but no score is ever 100% accurate to the performance it represents. If you listen closely you will hear all sorts of tiny timing differences and slight tuning issues in the original performance that haven't been captured on the score. **The original audio track is the standard by which any sequence is judged.** The skeleton score is just a helpful guide to get you started.

What is the examiner looking for?

The best way to find out the answer to this question is to look at the mark scheme. All examiners are trained how to apply the mark scheme to any work they are required to assess. In order to achieve the highest marks it is important for you to learn how to take a step back from your work and judge it according to the mark scheme criteria, just as an examiner would. Try for a second to distance yourself from all the hard work you have done and listen to the sequence with a critical ear. You may feel that, since you have put so much time into the work, examiners will be able to overlook the strange pitch clashes going on in bar 37, but they won't. Their job is to apply the mark scheme to every piece of music they hear in a fair and even-handed way, so all they care about is the quality of the audio they are listening to. Be your own harshest critic so that the deepest satisfaction comes from the knowledge that you have fulfilled your own extremely high expectations.

The mark scheme is split into four sections – accuracy of note input, mix, musicality and general music technology skills. Each section is subdivided into two criteria looking at specific aspects of the sequence.

The language used in the mark schemes makes more sense from an examiner's perspective than it will for someone who is actually doing the task, so the following is a paraphrase of the actual mark scheme.

It is possible to get zero marks in any criteria, but it is to be hoped that by reading this book you will avoid this possibility, so a mark of zero has not been addressed here.

1. Accuracy of note input

Pitch	8	Completely accurate. The sequence sounds just like the original track. There are no pitch errors at all.
	6 – 7	There may be a few pitch errors in the sequence. 7 marks would be awarded for where there are only two or three errors. 6 marks will be given when there are a few more errors, but the piece still sounds good. This category is used when there are errors, but they are tricky to spot.
	4 – 5	When there are more obvious errors that can easily be spotted or if there are repeated errors (such as a section which has been copied and pasted, but the original was wrong or an accidental has been consistently missed) the piece will fall into this category.
	2 – 3	When the errors start to make you cringe then the sequence will fall into this category.
	1	When only some of the track is accurate – there are more errors than there are correct notes, or there are sections of the piece which contain some very serious pitch problems.
Rhythm	8	Completely accurate. The sequence sounds just like the original track. There are no errors in rhythm input at all **and** the track sounds musical – there is a human feel to it rather than all the notes falling on the grid lines.
	6 – 7	The piece may be 100% accurate, but it feels a bit mechanical and unmusical: 7 marks. A few errors in the rhythm input, but these are quite hard to spot – they don't take anything away from the sequence.
	4 – 5	Errors are quite easily spotted, but the piece still sounds OK. If the different parts feel like they are playing out of time with each other then the sequence will fall into this category.
	2 – 3	Rhythmic errors make the sequence sound unmusical. There may be some serious errors that are repeated a lot (e.g. a repeated drum loop is wrong throughout in addition to some other rhythmic problems).
	1	When only some parts are accurate – there are problems in all or most parts.

Tuning is not marked in pitch – if there are tuning discrepancies between the original stimulus track and the skeleton score and you successfully sequence these in some way then you will gain credit in section 3 (Musicality) or 4 (Music Technology Skills), but you will not be penalised in pitch if they are not present. Any timing issues that are present in the original will be dealt with in the same way.

If parts are missing from your sequence then the examiners will penalise the piece in some way – they may mark as normal but take off a percentage according to how much is missing. **Do not** leave tracks out, even if they are tricky parts. The skeleton score will always have all the parts present in the piece listed in the first system of the music.

2. Choice and mix of sounds

Timbre	4	All the chosen sounds are very close to those used in the original track. Presets have been edited in some way to make them sound more like the original track. **Note:** You can only score 4 marks if there has been some editing of the preset sounds (refer to this in your log).
	3	All the chosen sounds are very close to those in the original track but there has been no editing of preset timbres. Or, there is some editing of presets, but there is the odd dodgy choice of timbre.
	2	Most of the sounds chosen are good, but there is the odd dodgy choice. Be particularly careful of your choice of sound for the vocal track or it is likely to fall into this category (avoid vocal or choral 'oohs' and 'aahs').
	1	There are several poor choices of timbre **or** the timbres chosen are in the same sort of family, but they sound nothing like those on the original track (e.g. synths have been chosen for the synth tracks, but they just don't come close to sounding like the original).
Balance and Pan	4	All the parts have been balanced and panned just like they are in the original track (including any odd balancing or panning in the original).
	3	The balance and panning are good, but may be different from the stimulus.
	2	There are some important parts that can't be clearly heard (e.g. some solo parts are too quiet or some background parts are too loud) and/or some of the parts have not been panned properly.
	1	There are several problems with the balance that make the sequence sound muddy or unclear and/or none of the parts have been panned.

The timbre category is marked according to the appropriate choice and editing of sounds. To some extent it is not important how good your sound module is, but you will have to do more editing to get the best from a poor quality sound source.

Make sure the instrumental parts are panned just like those in the original track. The mix should be like the original track as well, even if you think that one of the parts was a little loud or shouldn't have been panned the way it is.

3. Musicality

Dynamics	4	The dynamics are a faithful reproduction of the original and include volume swells etc. during notes (dynamic shaping) in addition to velocity changes.
	3	The main dynamic contrasts are present in the piece, but there are not many examples of dynamic shaping. Or there is a good deal of dynamic shaping etc., but it is not faithful to the original.
	2	It is clear that there has been some attempt to recreate the dynamics of the original, but there are some places where they are unsuccessful (e.g. crescendos and diminuendos are too sudden, grainy, or extreme).
	1	There has been some attempt to input dynamics, but most of those that have been programmed are either too subtle to have any effect or are unmusical (perhaps because they are too extreme or 'lumpy').
Articulation and Phrasing	4	The parts have been programmed so that they sound musical – the articulation and phrasing makes it sound like live musicians have performed them. Any of the obvious staccatos/legatos/tail-offs at the ends of phrases etc. of the original have been convincingly recreated in the sequence.
	3	Most of the phrasing of the original has been attempted but it is not entirely convincing or there is some musical phrasing and articulation, but it does not relate to the original track.
	2	There are clear attempts to edit the length, start times and relative strength of notes to create phrasing and articulation, but it sounds a little robotic.
	1	There has been little attempt to include any aspects of phrasing or articulation. Any attempts are either overly mechanical or actually take away from the success of the sequence (e.g. frequent evidence of very short staccato, notes audibly overlapping or unmusical pitch-bends).

It is particularly important to ensure that the vocal track or any main parts with exposed solos (e.g. a guitar solo) are carefully edited for musicality. Try to make the line 'sing' like the original through careful programming.

4. Music Technology Skills

Style and Creativity	4	A musical sequence. Any particular challenges posed by the stimulus material have been met. FX are appropriate and add to the piece. There is convincing use of pitch bend, modulation (vibrato) etc. to recreate elements of the original. Any tempo shaping adds to the piece. There is a feeling that the style of the original has been captured in the sequence.
	3	A consistent sense of style with some attention to musical detail resulting in a generally successful sequence.
	2	Where tempo shaping has been used, there may be one or two problems that have been introduced. FX have been used, but not always in a way that is suitable for the stimulus material. Some work has gone into editing the sequence, but it still doesn't really sound musical. A workmanlike attempt at making the piece sound like the original, but it hasn't quite hit the mark.
	1	The piece sounds quite robotic, with few obvious attempts to make it fit within the style. Any FX which are used are not really appropriate and, if tempo shaping has been used, it takes away from the success of the sequence rather than adding to it.
Quality of Recording	4	The final stereo recording has no blemishes in any way. The recording level is high without distorting and there is no evidence of clicks, hiss or clipping at any point in the track.
	3	There are one or two small blemishes in the final audio recording: e.g., it clips once or twice, there is a little hiss audible during silences or the playout is slightly too long. However, the recording is still good quality.
	2	There are several issues that take away from the success of the final recording: e.g., the beginning or ending may be chopped, there may be noticeable hiss throughout or it may distort occasionally.
	1	The final audio track is of poor quality. There may be a very long playout or a long silence at the beginning of the track or it may be mastered at a very low level.

> Style and creativity is a catch-all section for any aspects of sequencing which have not been dealt with elsewhere, such as appropriate use of FX, coping particularly well with a tricky guitar part, successfully programming a tempo change or matching the odd tuning discrepancy in a vocal part.

What are the rules for completing the task?

All practical work is to be completed under **controlled conditions**. There are certain rules you must adhere to in order to meet these conditions. Only the time you spend actually inputting, editing and mixing the actual sequence – **writing time** – falls under controlled conditions. Any time you spend preparing for the task falls outside of these conditions and is called **preparation time**.

'Preparation time' will include the following:

- O   Learning how to use the sequencing package
- O   Researching the stimulus material

- Analysing the stimulus material and learning the parts from the audio
- Transcribing parts of the stimulus material for later input
- Experimentation with sound sources in order to find appropriate timbres for the sequence
- Practising the parts on a MIDI instrument for later input into the sequencer
- Practising specific sequencing techniques (e.g. editing tempo maps or volume automation techniques) in order to apply these at a later stage to your sequence.

Any of the above may be undertaken in school/college or at home – it does not need to be directly supervised.

When you do any work to the file that will eventually be mixed down into a stereo track for submission to the examiner it is considered 'writing time', so you must observe the following rules:

1. All work must be your own. It is not acceptable to use any work that has been programmed by someone else (e.g. professional MIDI files or loops).
2. You must complete all the input, editing and mixing of the sequence under supervision by your teacher or another member of staff.
3. Your sequence must stay on the school/college premises at all times (you can't take it home or access it from home).
4. Any preparation work you bring into school/college must be checked by your teacher/supervisor before you restart 'writing time'.
5. You can access the internet during your preparation time, but not during inputting, editing and mixing of your sequence
6. You must complete the input, editing and mixing of the sequence within 20 hours (this does not include any preparation time).

How can I best use my time to complete the task?

Plan your time carefully!

There are 20 hours available to complete the input, editing and mixing of the sequencing task, so it needs to be used wisely. How you divide it up will depend on where your strengths and weaknesses lie as a music technologist. If you have good keyboard skills or are particularly good at playing tracks into a sequencer using a MIDI instrument then you will probably load your time towards data input – you will need to spend less time editing your sequence. If your strengths do not include keyboard skills then you will need a lot more time to edit your sequence in order to make it sound musical and to include the level of detail that is required to score top marks.

Data input

No matter how weak (or strong!) your keyboard skills are before you start the course, you are strongly advised to spend some time working on them so that you can play a simple melody with a good sense of musical phrasing (even if it is at a slow tempo). You will never be required to sight-read in this qualification or to perform with both hands playing simultaneous, independent parts, but you should spend some time learning to play a convincing tune with one hand. You don't have to be able to perform a Rachmaninov concerto!

It is possible to complete this task using a mouse to input the notes into a piano roll-style grid, but you may find it much more difficult to create the sense of musical phrasing required for the highest marks. A combination of playing in some parts and step-inputting others will probably be the best approach.

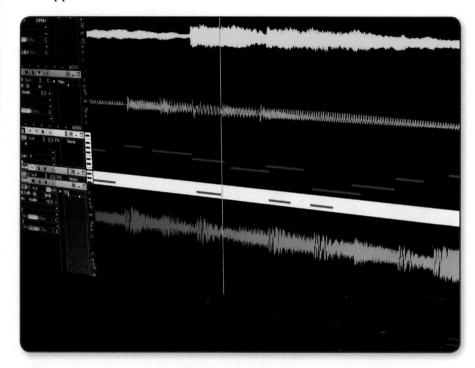

How can I make best use of the equipment available to me?

Learn how to use your software! Learn how to use your hardware!

At the start of the course you may have some time before the stimulus material is published. Do not waste this time. Experiment with the software your school/college has made available to you. Experiment with the sound sources available to you. Do not just play the sound sources in their normal range – experiment with them over the entire audible range and see how they respond to different controllers, pitch bend, different velocity levels and so on. Which types of sound are most realistic? Which timbres would need serious editing to make them sound good? Do you have a string sound that doesn't have a long attack time? Do you have a realistic distorted guitar sound? What sort of synth sounds do you have? Do certain timbres have pre-programmed effects? What effects do you have available? Will you need to make use of external effects in the audio domain instead of using the internal reverbs generated by the sound source? If so, ask your teacher how to go about doing this and experiment to see what results you can get. Learn how to use your plugins and automation facilities.

To summarise; learn the strengths and weakness of the equipment you have access to. Play to the strengths and learn how to overcome the weaknesses.

As you continue with your music technology career, either as a hobbyist or in a professional capacity, you will find that keyboard skills will come in handy, no matter how rudimentary they are.

Completing the sequencing task

- O   Preparation – transcription and practising parts
- O   Data input – acceptable software/sound sources, planning and inputting
- O   Editing
- O   Mixing – use of effects and mixing to stereo
- O   Completing the logbook.

Preparation

It is highly likely that if you are taking GCE Music Technology you have already put in quite a lot of preparation for some of the tasks you will undertake during the course.

Have you ever:

- O   Used a computer package of any sort to make music
- O   Learned to play piano or keyboard
- O   Worked out an interesting riff from listening to a CD
- O   Recorded something on any sort of portable recorder, computer or in a studio
- O   Rehearsed with a group of musicians
- O   Written a song either on your own or as part of a band
- O   Acted as a sound engineer at a live gig?

If you have ever taken part in any of these activities then you already have some of the skills in place that you will need to complete the Music Technology Portfolio. The more music making and creation you are involved in, the more honed your skills will become. For AS Music Technology you will hone some specific skills and target these so that the examiner can see the results of your efforts in the best possible light.

The first activity that falls under the umbrella of 'preparation time' proper is transcribing the audio for the sequence. Note that this can be completed under light supervision (your teacher should make regular checks of your progress) and it can be done either in your school/college or at home. Work at this stage can be taken into and out of the centre at any time.

Transcription

Immediately on publication of the stimulus material for Unit 1 you should start deciphering the audio track for the sequencing task. The act of writing down the parts from the audio track is called transcription. You do not need to produce a full score, and a great deal of the information will be on the skeleton score provided by Edexcel, so you do not have to do everything from scratch.

For some people, transcribing the audio material will be second nature as they frequently learn songs from CDs. For everyone else, there are a few techniques that will greatly speed up the process.

1) Become intimately familiar with the track

Listening to the track once or twice does not mean you know it. You should listen to it so that you can recognise every nuance of every part. Listen to the track a few times without any deep analysis (without reference to the skeleton score), then listen to the lead vocal, ignoring the other parts, then listen just to the drum track. Listen again to the synth and/or guitar parts. How many parts are there? Can you identify the effects on the different tracks? Listen to the production values of the track. What sort of reverb is on the snare? Are the drums far forward in the mix? Are there any backing vocals and, if so, how are they mixed? Is the timing metronomically accurate or does it groove? Does it microscopically anticipate the beat (it feels edgy) or does it almost imperceptibly lag behind the beat (it feels laid back). What type of bass guitar is used? Is the vocal double-tracked? These are the sorts of questions you should have all the answers to before you start writing out any music. Understanding the groove, style, instrumentation and structure of a song puts everything else into context and will inform many future decisions you make. You will know that you have absorbed the track properly when you can press the play button in your head and listen back all the way through without the assistance of a pair of speakers or headphones. Write down all your observations.

2) Build a framework

All music hangs together by means of a structure, no matter what the genre. Structure in music is like the framework on which everything else is built. With the aid of the skeleton score, write out the structure of the song. Put it in a table with sufficient space for the annotations to follow.

For example:

Intro

Verse 1

Chorus

Verse 2

Chorus

Instrumental

Chorus

Chorus

Now add the bar numbers for each of the sections as given in the skeleton score. Listen to the audio and count the bars and beats within the bars. Ensure you can hear where each section ends and the next begins.

Beside the bar numbers, add the timings of the sections in minutes and seconds:

Section	Bars	Timing
Intro	1–4	0'01"
Verse 1	5–12	0'09"
Chorus	13–20	0'25"

3) Identify where each instrument is used

1. Take a blank piece of A3 paper in landscape orientation – this is going to be a 'screenshot diagram' representing the arrange page of a sequencer
2. Rule a column down the left-hand side for the list of instruments
3. Rule a row across the top and bottom for bar and beat numbers
4. Rule a second row across the top for structure markings
5. Rule a series of vertical lines to represent bar numbers as appropriate to the length of the song (one vertical line per bar would be ideal) – if there is insufficient space then continue onto a second or third sheet of paper
6. Number every fourth bar in the row reserved for bar/beat numbers i.e. 1 – 5 – 9 – 13 and so on
7. Divide the sheet into rows, each of which represents one part as listed in the skeleton score
8. List the instruments down the left-hand column in the same order as they appear on the skeleton score
9. Transfer the information in your structure table to the second row of your sheet – you may wish to colour-code each section in this row
10. Make the barlines which separate the sections clear (perhaps by ruling in a different colour or with thicker lines)
11. By comparing to the skeleton score mark in the row reserved for the vocal track where the lead vocal actually sings – be very precise and thorough
12. Starting with the part you automatically gravitate to (if you are a drummer it is probably the drum part or, if a guitarist, the guitar part), listen carefully through the track and mark on the screenshot diagram where it plays

13. Repeat this process for the other parts being very careful to differentiate between like instruments i.e. if there are two synth parts, be careful not to mix the two up.

You should end up with a screenshot diagram containing information about the timings of every part used in the song. Ensure that you have left enough space to annotate further with more detailed information. See the example below:

BARS/BEATS	1	5	9	13	17	21	25	29	33	37	
STRUCTURE	INTRO				INTRO TWO		VERSE				
LEAD VOCAL							25:1				
BACKING VOCALS										39:1	
DRUM KIT			9:1 HI-HATS				23:4 FULL KIT				
PERCUSSION	1:1										
BASS	1:1										
KEYBOARD (CLAV)	1:1										
ELECTRIC GUITAR			9:1							39:1	
BRASS					16:3					40:1	
BARS/BEATS	1	5	9	13	17	21	25	29	33	37	

4) Start with what you know

Many of the important riffs and patterns have already been transcribed for you in the skeleton score. Develop a key to identify when these riffs and patterns occur on your screenshot diagram. For example, you might highlight the notated four-bar drum pattern in orange, so when this pattern is played in the song, highlight the appropriate space on your screenshot diagram in orange. If a second drum pattern is notated in the skeleton score, highlight this in a different colour and transfer the information to your screenshot diagram.

Again, start this process with the instrument you would normally gravitate to and repeat for the other parts. You may wish to write additional performance and/or production information in the appropriate spaces, for example: 'played aggressively' or 'slapback delay added'.

5) Fill in the blanks

There will be regions that have not been notated in the skeleton score you will have to work out for yourself. Develop a system of notating what you hear – this does not have to be staff notation. You may simply learn the parts on the keyboard and keep the notation very simple as a memory aid. Some may find it easiest to start with a line representing the melodic contour that can be gradually refined to represent the individual pitch names. If you struggle to notate rhythm, just learn to clap or tap the rhythms at a given point and use some form of shorthand as a memory aid (perhaps a series of dots, dashes, spaces and lines). Remember that some parts do not always have a clearly defined pitch, especially when considering certain styles of vocal delivery, so some graphic notation may actually be the best way to notate examples of this. You may be able to directly transfer the graphic notation to performance on the pitch bend wheel.

It will be best to transcribe parts on a separate sheet of paper, only transferring to the screenshot diagram written annotations about performance/production detail along with a key to represent where each riff or pattern occurs.

Practising

Learn as many parts as you can on the keyboard, particularly exposed or solo parts such as the main vocal line or a guitar solo. You do not have to be able to play it up to speed but, if you slow it down, remember to slow down **all** of the part proportionately (don't play the tricky bar slowly and the rest up to speed). Practise the parts in short phrases that make musical sense. Practising the parts on the keyboard is still part of 'preparation time', so it will make life much easier when it comes to data input and editing (which falls under 'writing time') if you have learned to play some parts accurately and musically.

Data input

Any data input must be completed under supervision – it cannot be done outside the school/college. Work cannot be taken out of the centre and you must not access the internet while working on your sequencing file. It is perfectly acceptable to split preparation and writing time into blocks – you do not have to complete all your preparation and then 'start the clock' for the writing time. It may be best to practise small sections as preparation and then input these sections under supervision, then repeat the process for other sections.

It is not acceptable to use audio in this task in any way, except in the form of single-hit samples (see below for more information on appropriate sound sources). Audio loops can only be used if clearly stated in the rubric on the front cover of the stimulus material for Music Technology Portfolio 1, otherwise they must not be used at any point in the sequence. The voice part for the song must be sequenced using an appropriate instrumental timbre – it must not be a live audio recording of the vocal part.

What software is acceptable?

Edexcel neither recommends nor prohibits the use of any sequencing software. The specification states that 'a computer-based sequencing program' should be used (paragraph 1, page 25) and the Getting Started guide has the following to say about software choice:

'There is no set restriction on which software may be used for the completion of Task 1A. However, students will be significantly disadvantaged if they are not able to access a full range of facilities with which to edit their pitch, rhythm and controller data. It is possible to use a range of different software packages for different stages of the task as long as all the work is the unaided work of the candidate.'

(Edexcel GCE Music Technology, Getting Started: page 9)

This means that it is possible to use any sequencing software that suits your working style as long as you are able to edit data appropriately. It would be acceptable to input notes in one package and then export to another for editing. It would also be acceptable to input one type of track (e.g. drums) in one package and export into the main file. This is not necessarily to be recommended as there may be some synchronisation or transfer issues introduced, over-complicating the task.

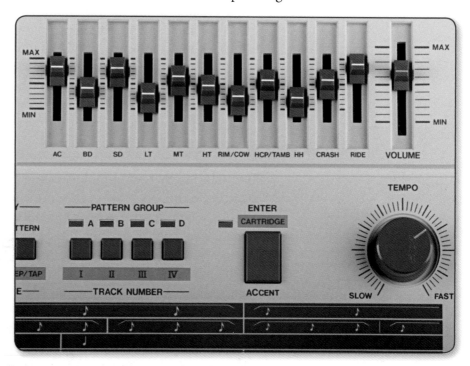

The specification states that you '… may use a range of available sound sources and programming techniques. These could include GM (General MIDI) soundsets, hardware/software sound modules and synthesisers, audio loops and samples, virtual studio instruments and sample libraries.' (last paragraph, page 25). However, as mentioned earlier, audio loops may only be used if explicitly stated on the front cover of the stimulus material published by Edexcel for the year of your examination. There is no guarantee that if audio loops are allowed one year, they will be allowed the next. Stay clear of using loops unless you are 100% certain that the stimulus material says you are allowed to use them. Other than this, most other sound sources are acceptable.

- ○ GM soundsets – these are available on most sound modules and sound cards, but may not be the best quality sounds available. They provide the 'bread-and-butter' sounds that are in common use.
- ○ Hardware sound modules – these are standalone boxes that

connect to a keyboard or computer by means of a cable (MIDI, USB, FireWire etc.) and need to have their audio outputs connected to a mixing desk or headphones in order to hear the sounds produced.

O Synthesisers – a piano keyboard in the same casing as a sound module. These often have options to add expansion cards for additional sounds and generally allow significant editing of sounds within the host environment or specific sound generation facilities. Many synthesisers now offer connection options to computers for on-screen editing and can often connect by means of a USB cable.

O Software sound modules/virtual studio instruments – these are often software versions of existing technology e.g. a plugin mimicking the Hammond B3 drawbar organ, but they may be completely original instruments that make use of the processing power of a host computer to produce sounds hardware synths are incapable of. The output of these will normally be routed internally using a drop-down menu in the host sequencer.

O Samples and sample libraries – short audio recordings of real-life sounds. These will only be acceptable for the sequencing task if they consist of individual hits which can be edited in similar ways to a GM or synthesiser sound. Sample libraries contain sets of samples programmed across the range of the keyboard and layered so that different velocities produce different timbral characteristics. Many drum sets consist of sampled, individual hits.

Bear in mind that the stimulus track may be a song which used very basic synth timbres itself, so in some cases you will have an easier job editing quite primitive sounds to get the correct timbre than using the latest, all singing, all dancing piece of kit available.

Planning

In any pop song there will be a significant amount of repetition. On your screenshot diagram, map out which parts can be directly copied and pasted and which parts can be copied and pasted with a little additional editing. **Do not** copy and paste anything until you have double-checked it for accuracy of note input and edited it for interpretative detail or you will give yourself a great deal of extra work to do.

Inputting

Everyone has their own working methods, but the following is an example of a method which is tried and tested:

1) Import the original stimulus audio into an audio track

Create a stereo audio track in your sequencer and import the original stimulus audio. The audio will normally begin from where the playhead is positioned ('now time' or position you have reached in the song). Be aware that if you start the audio from beat 1 bar 1, there may be issues with too much data being sent on the very first note when you input all your sequencing data and any header files. Check this in a test run before you start inputting the task. If you decide to start the audio from a different bar make sure that you adjust the bar numbers in the screenshot diagram to match.

The audio track will act as a guide to the rest of your inputting and editing activities. It must be muted or deleted before mixing the sequence down to the final stereo audio file.

2) Create additional tracks to match the parts listed in your screenshot diagram

Exactly how you go about this will depend on your choice of software and sound source(s). If you are using a sequencer with an external sound module this will involve creating a number of MIDI tracks equal to the number of parts you have previously listed in the screenshot diagram and directing the MIDI output of the track to the MIDI input of your sound module. If you are using software instruments then you will need to open an instance of the software instrument and direct the output of the track to that instrument. Before going any further, ensure that you are getting the sound you require from each track and that you have assigned different MIDI channels to each track as appropriate. You should try to select the appropriate timbre for each track before you start inputting the notes so that you can get an idea of how you might need to edit the sequence as you go along.

3) Create a tempo map to exactly match the stimulus audio

The stimulus audio will be at the tempo given in the skeleton score. However, it is rare for a piece of recorded music to remain at the same tempo throughout the song, so you will need to frequently update the tempo of your sequence so that it matches the tempo of the original track at any given moment. This is best done in the graphical tempo editor of your sequencing package (normally called the tempo track or view). Some packages have a preset algorithm that automatically matches the tempo of the sequence to the tempo of any audio tracks or loops. While the specification does not expressly forbid the use of such functions, the general rule of thumb is that you can only gain credit for anything which you have programmed yourself (and backed up with a comment in the logbook), so be careful when deciding to use preset tempo maps. Also, trying to set a preset algorithm to map across a three-minute-plus track may introduce some errors.

i. Set the initial tempo to that given in the skeleton score.
ii. Turn on the metronome (setting it to be audible in playback mode) and play the sequence. If the metronome seems to be slightly out of time with the audio track, adjust accordingly (you may need to make very fine adjustments, sometimes less than 1 bpm).
iii. Once you have established the basic tempo for the track, play through until the metronome seems to be even the tiniest fraction out of sync with the audio track. Mark this point, but let the sequence continue playing until it is clear whether the tempo needs to be faster or slower, then adjust accordingly at the place you previously marked. This will take some experimentation and patience.
iv. Continue this process until you reach the end of the audio.

There are several points to bear in mind when creating a tempo map:

○ The tempo often speeds up fractionally in the chorus and slows down again when returning to the verse

○ Sometimes the tempo changes are gradual, so will require more than one change over a period of a few bars to keep the sequence in time with the original (you may draw a line to represent a gradual change rather than inputting several discrete changes)

○ Tempo changes are not always linear – you may achieve a better result drawing in a curve rather than a straight line

○ In some songs the tempo doesn't change at all

○ Sometimes a song has a particular groove, or may even have one groove for one section and then change for the next. This may give the impression of tempo changes where they do not really exist – to sequence the groove accurately you may need to edit the start times of some of the notes so they come fractionally before or after the gridlines in your edit window

○ Overdoing tempo changes can ruin an otherwise excellent sequence – be careful!

4) Input the drum part

Refer to the notes you made previously on the drum track. Did you feel it was edgy or laid back? If it felt edgy, as if it was always pushing the track then at least some of the drum hits will fall marginally before the beat. If it felt laid back, some of the hits will fall marginally after the beat. If it felt programmed and mechanical then the hits were probably directly on the beat and may have had minimal or predictable velocity editing. From listening to the track, decide whether it would be best to play the drum part in using a MIDI keyboard or MIDI drum pads (perhaps in several takes, building up the elements of the kit with each subsequent take) or whether the stimulus needs a rock-solid, mechanically accurate rhythm part, in which case it would be better to program it in using a drum editor and a mouse.

This demonstrates the tightrope you have to walk when sequencing – you normally want the piece to sound like it was played live (it has a 'human' feel to it), but you want it to sound rhythmically tight (as if it was played by someone with a seriously good sense of timing). Deliberately introducing timing errors can often lead to a very messy sounding track, but programming everything on the gridlines will lead to a very mechanical sounding track. Often the best way around this is to have a very tight rhythm section and a looser, more 'human' lead line, but each song will call for a unique approach.

On the beat

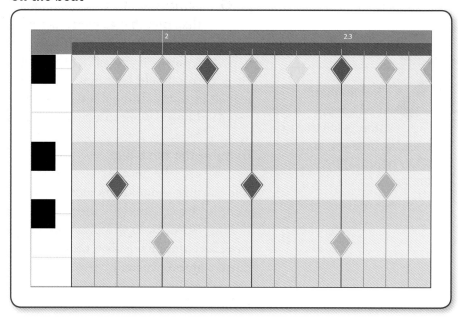

Slightly after the beat – a laid back feel

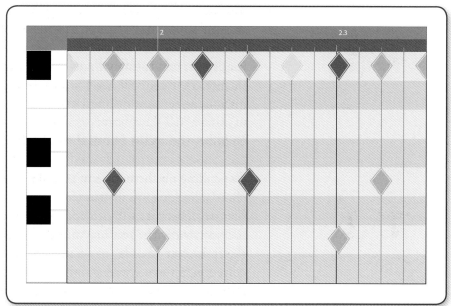

Slightly before the beat – an edgy feel

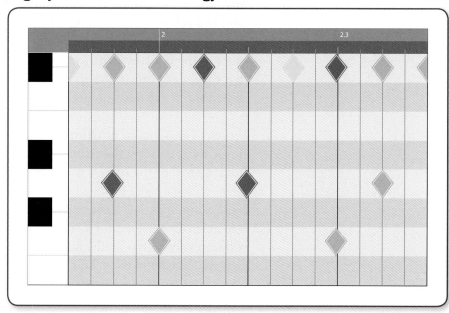

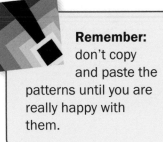

Remember: don't copy and paste the patterns until you are really happy with them.

Input the drum part in logical sections as dictated by your screenshot diagram. Do not try to input long sections all in one go. You may wish to begin with the basic patterns, leaving fills for later.

By now you should have developed the habit of saving your work at regular intervals. This habit will become deeply ingrained if you lose a couple of hours' work to a computer crash.

5) Input the bass line

The bass line should work alongside the drum track. If you listen to any recorded band, especially those which are considered to have a 'tight' rhythm section, you will hear that the kick drum and the bass guitar work very closely together, often falling at exactly the same time or laying down a groove where the two are very closely related and are dependent on each other. As such, the bass line should be inputted either along with the drum part or immediately after you have finished the drum part, and should be considered as part of the rhythm section. Most of the comments for point 4 will therefore hold true for inputting the bass part.

In addition to the rhythmic qualities of the bass, it should be remembered that bass notes sustain and can be manipulated at any point along the note's duration (using vibrato, slides, bends and so on). Listen for any nuances that you will need to add during the editing stage and note them on your screenshot diagram or in your general notes.

6) Input the main chordal backing/main riff

Depending on the nature of the stimulus material, there will be either a chordal backing, an instrument playing a main riff, or a combination of the two. This part will provide the harmonic meat for the rhythm and melody sandwich. You may need to interpret chord symbols given in the skeleton score in order to accurately input this part. However, getting the correct notes in a chord is only half the battle; the other half is to put the notes in a suitable order. For example, the 'Hendrix chord' (E7♯9) sounds great on a guitar when you know the chord shape, but if you play the notes in any order on the keyboard (E, G, G♯, B, D) it can sound terrible. Try playing the notes on a keyboard in the following order, somewhere around middle C (from bottom to top): E – G♯ – B – D – G. Nice and jazzy, if a little crunchy. Now try E – G – B – D – G♯ (reversing the order of the G natural and G sharp). Not so pleasant. This demonstrates that the order of the notes in a chord (or the 'voicing') is particularly important in extended or altered chords.

If there is an acoustic or strummed guitar part, it may be best to save this whole part until the editing stage as the editing is probably more fundamental to the success of the part than the actual pitches.

Some songs have less harmonic filling and depend on a riff to fulfil the role normally reserved for a strummed guitar or keyboard chords. This riff will normally be repeated a lot, but will probably include frequent, small changes. Be careful to include all these changes and avoid being lulled into a false sense of security if the riff has remained unchanged for ten repetitions.

7) Input other important accompaniment parts

Now that you have input the basic track, you can begin to add the other accompaniment parts. Make sure they sound in time with the tracks you have programmed thus far. Double check your track against the original audio with the addition of each part and listen with a critical ear as you go along (while staying within your time schedule). Leave the additional 'ear candy' tracks – those that make cameo appearances for production values – until after you have programmed the vocal line.

8) Input the vocal line

This is the most important part to get right, so leave sufficient time for it. However, do not spend all your time in the tiny detail when there are still tracks missing – be conscious of your time budget.

By far the best way to input the vocal part is to play it in. Practise each individual phrase (you can spend as long as is required doing this as preparation time) and, when each phrase is perfect, play it into the sequencer. It is very likely that you will have to use a fair amount of pitch bend to emulate the tuning discrepancies of the performer, or to slide between notes. You can either directly include this in your performance of the track or you could add pitch bend data to the track by playing the pitch bend wheel in a subsequent take.

The choice of timbre for the vocal line will have a major impact on the success, not just of this one part, but of the whole sequence. You should select a sound in keeping with the quality of the original vocal part – e.g. raunchy, pure, crystalline, dark, breathy. However, this choice should be tempered by the selection of instruments in the main sequence. If the instrumental tracks include a saxophone then you should not use a saxophone for the vocal part: the two would inhabit the same sonic space and would fight against rather than complement each other. Similarly, if there are synth sounds in a song, it may be appropriate to use a sawtooth wave for the vocal, but it would have to be sufficiently different from the other synth sounds in the main track in order to sit well in the mix. Pseudo-vocal sounds such as choral or vocal 'oohs' and 'aahs' or scat should be avoided. The timbre chosen should have a voice-like quality to it, i.e., it should be able to change throughout the duration of a note and not fade in or out (except when required). It should be able to 'sing' over the top of the other sequenced tracks.

9) Add any major instrumental solos/exposed instrumental parts

Major instrumental breaks (such as guitar solos) are on a similar level to lead vocal parts, so the issues raised in point 8 will apply here too.

10) Add any additional, minor parts and production elements

The last bells and whistles can be saved for the end, but do leave enough time for these parts as missing tracks will be penalised by the examiner. Be aware of the importance of these pieces of 'ear candy' – they are there to make the piece sound interesting, but they supplement and support the main act – the lead vocal. Your sequence should sound this way (unless the stimulus track contradicts this statement in which case you should always go with the audio).

11) Check against the original audio

At frequent intervals during the input process, you should check what you have programmed against the reference audio track. It is especially important to double check the accuracy of a part before and after you copy and paste it. Check the accuracy beforehand so that you don't have to edit it twice, and check afterwards just in case there was a slight change in the audio when the part is repeated that you hadn't noticed before.

Editing

All editing of the sequencing task should be completed under controlled conditions.

Timbre

> Remember that many preset sounds have effects added to make them sound as impressive as possible on a casual glance while browsing in a shop, so you may have to do more removing of unwanted effects than addition of wanted ones.

It is more important to show that you have chosen and edited appropriate sounds than it is to have the best sounds available. When we looked at the mark scheme you saw that it is only possible to score three marks out of four for a good choice of timbres. To get into the top category it is essential to have edited at least some of the chosen sounds. It is likely that you will have to edit the timbre chosen for the lead vocal sound to get it just the way you want it, so this will be a good start.

Choose timbres that are close to the original sounds to begin with and then edit the EQ, the attack and decay, the amount of resonance and filter cutoff and add **or take away** effects as appropriate. If you are using a very basic soundset, experiment with layering multiple sounds with different volume levels to see if you can improve on the basic palette you have available.

List all the details of timbre editing in your logbook. Even if there is no official space to mention what you have done, either add a note at the bottom of question 1 in the logbook or include an extra sheet detailing your efforts. Label it 'Timbre Editing'.

Balance, pan and dynamics

Dynamics processing (using compressors, limiters, etc.) alters the dynamic range of recordings – it will be looked at in Unit 1B. Use of the word 'Dynamics' as relates to sequencing is always referring to the musical dynamics (*p*, *sf*, *cresc*. etc).

Balance and pan (and to some extent, dynamics and reverb) are interrelated. If parts are panned appropriately, they will not fight each other as much for sonic space, so there is less likelihood of balance problems occurring. Similarly, if background sounds have a suitable type and amount of reverb added, they will fit into the mix better.

Dynamics are the changes in volume that occur in the performance of an individual part: for example a note might be suddenly loud, followed by a steep diminuendo and a gradual crescendo. Balance is the overall volume of a part relative to the other parts sounding at the same time. So, the dynamics described above may be present in a part which is either loud or quiet relative to the other parts playing at the same time.

This distinction between balance and dynamics is one of the reasons for the distinction between the controllers CC7 (Main Channel Volume) and CC11 (Expression). CC7 has traditionally been used to set the balance between instruments – it is used in the same way as a fader on a mixing desk and CC11 has been used to control the individual dynamics within a part. However, the two controllers have the same end result in that they both alter the volume of a part, so it is up to you and your teacher how you decide to approach this issue. You should be aware of what each of the controllers do, but you do not necessarily have to use them. As sequencing software progresses, the methods of editing become more powerful and more subtle in many ways. All the major sequencers offer a mixer view that allows you to edit the volume of a track in a visual way, much like a mixing desk (even in the MIDI domain). Generally these faders will map to CC7 (they will alter the Main Channel Volume of any attached MIDI device on this MIDI channel), but it depends on your sound source. For this task the important thing is to edit the dynamics and balance regardless of what editing options you use to do so. It is also possible to edit the dynamics and balance directly on the main arrange window of most major sequencers by drawing automation curves. This approach is equally valid to using controller lanes in an edit window in which you draw curves to alter CC7 or CC11.

If you do use one controller or one volume control to adjust both balance and dynamics, be aware that you cannot adjust one without changing the other.

Another important method of editing dynamics is to change the velocity of individual notes. The velocity value is the same for the whole duration of a note, so it is not suitable for volume swells during a note (remember that you can only score full marks for dynamics if you have included some dynamic shaping), but it can be very useful for adding life to drum and piano parts for which changes in volume during the note may sound unnatural. Another aspect of velocity is that many sound sources are programmed to play back a different quality of timbre according to the velocity level. For example, a trombone sound played at a very low velocity level may give a sweet, round sound, but a high velocity level may result in a very different, harsher, brassy timbre. You would not be able to access this 'velocity layering' just by using volume automation or controller changes.

Be wary of extreme dynamic contrasts – these can take more away from a sequenced performance than they add to it. Only use extremes if you are sure the original audio track warrants it.

Parts should be panned across the stereo field exactly as they are in the original audio track. Copy the audio, even if you disagree with some of the original settings. If you think something is extremely odd for example, everything is coming out of one speaker), check your connections, the orientation of your headphones and that the original audio transferred onto a stereo track (which is panned hard left and hard right). It may be best to pan the tracks appropriately before adjusting the balance as this may have an impact on the perceived level of parts.

Articulation and phrasing

As mentioned in the data input section, natural sounding phrasing is much easier to achieve by playing it in rather than programming it after data input. Phrasing is a combination of velocity levels, very precise timing information, note duration, volume shaping, pitch information and the relationship of one note to another, placing all the notes in context. Due to the interaction of these elements, there are few hard and fast rules about what aspect you should alter to achieve a certain effect. It is true that if notes overlap slightly they will give a legato (smooth) effect and if they are approximately half their normal length they will sound staccato (detached). However, giving a phrase a sense of shape requires much more subtle interplay between the elements. Try to practise phrases as a whole and play them into the sequencer, correcting mistakes such as notes that overlap too much or incorrect pitches afterwards as part of the editing process. If you absolutely have to input everything with a mouse, try to study how a good performer uses the elements listed above to achieve a sense of phrasing and use the editing tools at your disposal to get as close to this as you can.

Articulation is closely related to phrasing, but it is much easier to achieve after data input than is the case with phrasing. In general, articulation refers to the way a note is sounded: i.e., accented, staccato, slurred or unaltered. An accent would best be achieved by programming a higher velocity for that note than for those surrounding it.

Style and creativity

Use of effects, pitch bend and tempo changes will contribute to the sense of style in a sequence. As with any other editing processes, they should be used subtly and should be present only to recreate what is in the original audio track.

A sense of style is also related to the phrasing and groove of a track – if you have managed to capture the laid back groove of a rhythm section by programming the drums appropriately then you will have gone some distance to displaying a good sense of style. Appropriate use of pitch bend to recreate the tuning and scooping to and from notes as evidenced in the vocal track will gain credit in this section of the mark scheme.

Keep checking your work against the original audio (and the skeleton score/your screenshot diagram). Remember to periodically save your work.

Mixing

Refer to **Editing,** point (2) for detail on balance and pan.

Use of effects

Reverb and delay are the most likely effects that you will need to use in task 1A. It is possible that there may be the need for some chorus on a fretless bass or clean guitar sound, but most tracks will require reverb of some sort and some tracks will need a little delay. It is unlikely that

sounds produced in a sound module, sound card, plugin or synth will require any dynamics processing.

It is acceptable to export parts individually as audio to be processed through an audio effects processor after they have been completed, but be aware of the timing issues which may arise as a result of doing so and the fact that the parts cannot be further edited once they are in the audio domain.

CC91 is the controller responsible for reverb depth in the MIDI domain, but many plugins will have their own reverb engines built-in. Be careful not to stack incompatible reverbs on top of one another – for example, if a sound has a pre-programmed hall reverb with a lot of high frequency content, avoid adding another reverb on top of this with a very short reverb tail, lots of early reflections and a totally different EQ setting as it is likely to confuse the mix. Also, be aware of how any added reverb effects the stereo placement of each track. Refer to the notes you made originally about what type of reverb is used on which tracks. Listen again to the original audio to check how much reverb depth might need to be applied to each part.

Delay is much more difficult to achieve in the MIDI domain. Several sequencers do have a special MIDI effects section, emulating audio effects in the MIDI domain, so you may wish to check this out. A rather unsubtle method of applying a delay-like effect to a MIDI track is to duplicate the part to be delayed. Send the duplicate part to a different MIDI channel and reduce the high frequency EQ quite a lot. Set the level of this part considerably lower than the original and shift the start time so that it is 'delayed' by the required amount. Moving it by a very short amount will have a 'thickening' effect on the original part, while moving it by a beat will give the effect of a timed delay. A 'U2' style guitar echo would be achieved by shifting the duplicate by three quarters of a beat. Remember that, by adding another occurrence of the original part you will be increasing its perceived level considerably in the mix. Be careful of the placement of the delayed part to avoid confusing the stereo image. Repeating the process outlined above would produce additional repeats for the delay effect.

A double-tracking effect would be best achieved by playing the part in twice, just like you would if you were recording live. Note that this would not work if you were inputting using a mouse! Again, be careful of the overall levels of the part when it is double-tracked and that any edits are carried out on both parts.

Mixing to stereo

How you go about this will depend on the sound source you have used. If you have used an external sound module or synth then you will need to route them through a mixer to a CD burner or other suitable recording device. If you are using internal sounds and/or plugins, the sequencing package will offer methods of mixing the sequence to audio. This process must be completed within the overall 20-hour time limit, so it is important to become familiar with the process before undertaking it for the task. Any technical problems can be dealt with outside of controlled conditions.

Before you mix to the final stereo audio track, double-check that you are happy with all aspects of the sequence. It is always best to leave things for a while (perhaps a week or more) before completing this final stage so that you can come back to the task and listen to it with fresh ears. When you have reached the stage that you feel you have done everything you can do then go onto another task for a while before coming back to this one to confirm you are happy with it.

Check your work against the mark scheme given earlier in this chapter. Try to apply it as objectively as possible. If you can think of any ways of improving your work when relating it to the mark scheme, do so before mixing down.

There are several aspects to consider in order to achieve the highest marks for 'Quality of recording':

- The lead-in should be no more than two seconds
- Notes should not be cut off at the start or end of the audio track
- The original audio track (if used as a guide) should be muted or deleted when mixing the sequence to audio
- Distortion or clipping must be avoided while maintaining a high overall recording level
- There should be no clicks, hiss, noise or other artefacts introduced to the audio when mixing to stereo
- Any reverb tail at the end of the sequence should decay naturally
- Any fade out should be smooth
- Any silence at the end of the fadeout/reverb tail should not exceed two seconds.

Check the final audio mix after it has been saved as a WAV file or burnt to CD. Compare it to other recordings to check the overall level and listen carefully for any evidence of the areas listed above.

Well done – you have completed task 1A! Now complete your log for the task.

Completing the logbook

Questions 1 and 2 of the logbook refer to task 1A and simply ask for details of any equipment used and any samples present in the sequence (if appropriate). The two questions do not attract any marks, but it is vital that you complete the information or the work may not be assessed. It is also in your best interests to include any additional information you feel may assist the examiner in assessing your sequence, especially concerning any work done in editing timbres and effects. Keep any additional information brief and to the point – there is no need to write any long, rambling essays. Refer to anything that isn't obvious by just listening to the final result: remember that the only information the examiner has is the final audio mixdown and the information in your logbook. Make sure you get the credit you deserve!

What does the task entail?

This task is all about trying to produce a recording that is of the highest possible quality. Unlike the sequencing task, you do not have to try and replicate a professional recording in every detail (although this may be a good starting point for your ambitions), but you do have to ensure that each stage of the recording process – the capture, the processing and the mixing of the tracks – is as close to a professional standard as you can manage.

You are expected to be in charge of every stage of the recording process, from the setting up of microphones to the final mixing down to a stereo track. This can be an exciting and interesting task, but it does require careful forethought and planning in order to be successful.

For this task, the golden rule is to ensure that you do not take on too ambitious a project – you must take care of the small details in order to make the big picture look good.

Examiners are looking for quality, not quantity. They want to hear a well-balanced mix with appropriate use of effects and processors enhancing well-captured audio tracks. They do not want to hear a 40-track, mega-multi-tracked extravaganza in which nothing can be made out from the wall of sound that is your final mix. In this task one of the dangers is that you get used to the sound of your own recording, missing aspects that are in serious need of attention. Take regular breaks from your work, revisiting it with fresh ears. Frequently compare your work to that of any mixes you are seeking to recreate and be brutally honest in your self-evaluation. Do not make excuses for any poor quality work – instead, find out what the problem is and do everything you can to fix it.

It is important to forget about your own instrumental preferences – for example, if you are a guitarist, you must not be tempted to put guitars to the fore at the expense of the overall mix. Take care at each stage of the process to get everything sounding just right. Although the 'fix it in the mix' approach is becoming increasingly possible as audio recording packages introduce more and more powerful editing facilities, it is still best to avoid the time and effort this will take by getting everything right in the first place.

The mark scheme is divided into three sections, each focussing on one stage of the recording process. These are subdivided as necessary to focus on the individual elements that make up each stage. It is important to recognise that several of these areas are interdependent – for example, how well you have panned the individual tracks and your use of reverb will have an impact on the balance and blend of a recording. The following is a paraphrase of the mark scheme in the specification.

1. Capture

Microphone Placement and Clarity of Signal	6	All mics have been chosen appropriately for the instrument or voice they are being used to capture. All tracks have been captured clearly. There are no problems arising as a result of poor mic positioning.
	4 – 5	All mics are appropriate for the task. There may be one or two problems arising from mic placement not being quite right, but the capture is generally good.
	2 – 3	Most of the choices of mic are appropriate for the task, but there are a few that are not suitable for what they are being used to capture. Several parts have not been recorded well: e.g., there might be too much hi-hat on the snare drum track making proper balance and processing impossible, or the acoustic guitar may have been recorded too close to the fretboard resulting in too much finger squeak and a thin sound.
	1	There is a lack of clarity in the recording introduced as a result of choosing the wrong mics for the task and/or poor placement of the mics. The captured sound is poor from the outset.
Noise and Distortion	5	Only the desired signal has been captured – there is no noise, distortion, clipping or thudding on any of the tracks. There is an excellent signal to noise ratio and any background sound has been eliminated.
	3 – 4	Most of the tracks have been recorded well, but there is the odd noise that has made its way onto the final recording (e.g. a mic stand thud, a background noise or a very slight hiss). None of these extraneous noises are very obvious – you would have to listen carefully to hear them.
	2	Some obvious noises have made their way onto the recording. The gain level may have been much too high or low during sound capture resulting in distortion or excess, intrusive hiss.
	1	Unacceptably noisy and poorly made recording.

You are not expected to be Trevor Horn at this stage of your career, so don't try to replicate his complex mixes – you are just expected to do the basics well.

All recordings are expected to have a short and noise free lead-in and out. If this is not the case, it would be penalised under 'Noise and Distortion'.

2. Processing

Management of EQ	6	The recording boasts a full frequency range, from full and tight bass frequencies to high transient sounds. No points on the frequency spectrum are boomy, boxy, nasal, harsh, or overly bright.
	4 – 5	The frequency range has been well reflected in the recording, but there are a few areas or tracks that could benefit from additional EQing. There may be two tracks inhabiting similar frequency ranges (e.g. two electric guitars or synths) that could do with more separation, but any EQ problems are minor.
	2 – 3	Some tracks need additional EQ to sit properly in the mix. There are some clear problems in the frequency range that have not been attended to. There may be one track that really causes problems for the whole mix (e.g. a dominant, muddy bass).
	1	No EQ has been used or, when it has been used, it has been used badly, making the track sound worse than it did before processing.
Management of Dynamics	6	Excellent use of compression and limiter (where appropriate) so that all the tracks have a consistent volume throughout. There are no audible side effects of compression (such as 'pumping') and the use of dynamics processing has helped all the tracks to sit well in the mix. The dynamics have been processed in a way that is suitable for the style of the song.
	4 – 5	Compression has been used well in the recording, but one or two tracks may be a touch lifeless due to overuse, or one or two tracks may stand out in the mix because they haven't been processed properly. Any misuse of dynamics processing is audible but not intrusive.
	2 – 3	Dynamics processing has been applied in an inconsistent way. There may be inappropriate use of compression/limiter/expander/gate that causes some tracks to be dull and lifeless or to leap out of the mix. The misuse of dynamics processing is intrusive.
	1	There is very little use of dynamics processing or, when it is used, it makes the track sound worse than it did before processing.
Effects/Ambience	6	Effects have been used carefully and effectively, as appropriate to the style of the music to enhance the recording. All the effects used have been well chosen.
	4 – 5	The effects used have been mostly well chosen as appropriate to the style of the music. There may be the odd instance where a track is slightly too dry or wet, but it does not take away from the recording.
	2 – 3	Effects have been used in the track, but there may be some poor choices or two or more tracks are too dry or wet, noticeably detracting from the quality of the recording.
	1	Many of the tracks are far too dry or wet, significantly detracting from the quality of the recording. Several effects may have been poorly chosen.

It is not necessary to use limiters, expanders and gates to gain full marks for dynamics processing at AS level – appropriate use of compression will be sufficient.

Reverb is the most important effect to get right. Novelty effects (such as a global, two octave pitch shift) should be avoided. Sometimes an ambience setting will be enough to give a track a sense of space. You should experiment with the settings on the reverb unit rather than just accepting presets. Different tracks will require different effects applied at different levels. 'Dry' refers to the original, unaffected signal. 'Wet' refers to the effected signal.

3. Mixing

Balance and Blend	6	All the tracks are mixed well, giving an excellent overall sound. Everything is balanced as appropriate to the style, with all the parts audible and at the expected level. If parts are meant to blend in together, they do so and if they are meant to stand out, they do so.
	4 – 5	Most of the tracks have been well balanced. There may be a few moments where something is not as loud or soft as it needs to be or there are a few areas where parts do not blend as well as they could, but the mix is generally successful.
	2 – 3	The mix works from time to time, but often there are areas where parts do not blend in together or there are times when important parts (e.g. lead vocals or instrumental solos) are lost in the mix. Some tracks may be far too quiet (e.g. very quiet drums result in the song lacking drive) or far too loud.
	1	The mix really takes away from the success of the recording. There are many areas where parts are lost or drown everything else out. Tracks do not blend well.
Use of Stereo Field	5	The track has a real sense of width with all the tracks panned appropriately. The panning adds to the sense of space without leaving any big gaps in the middle.
	3 – 4	Good use has been made of the stereo field with few misjudgements in where the parts have been placed. The sense of stereo may not be as wide as it could be or there may be a bit of a hole in the middle.
	2	There are some errors in where tracks have been placed in the stereo field (e.g. strong parts are misplaced or unbalanced resulting in a sense of one side being more dominant than the other). The stereo field may feel restricted.
	1	Very little (or no) use has been made of the stereo field or there are some very serious errors in where instruments have been placed.

Although the specification mark scheme mentions 'creative' in the use of stereo field section, it does not mean that you should use panning in a new and original way, rather it means that you have creatively solved mixing problems using panning. It is better just to stick to a safe and sure, musically appropriate panning setup rather than trying to be overly creative.

What are the rules for completing the task?

The multi-track recording must be completed under controlled conditions.

For the multi-track recording, 'preparation time' will include the following:

- Choosing suitable material to record
- Researching the style – listening to a wide range of tracks within this style
- Listening to mixes in the chosen style, analysing how effects and processors have been used and where instruments are placed in the mix
- Learning how to use the microphones and equipment
- Learning how to use the multi-track recording device/program
- Organising musicians to play the selected material
- Rehearsing musicians to a suitable standard
- Experimenting with microphone choice and placements for each of the instruments/vocals
- Soundchecking and testing equipment
- Level setting.

Most of the above can be undertaken at home or in school/college, without being supervised, but the placement of mics and level setting, while not falling under the time limitations of controlled conditions, would have to be completed under supervision.

Any recording work that will eventually be mixed down into a stereo track for submission to the examiner is considered to be 'writing time', so you must observe the following rules:

1. All stages of the recording process must be under your own personal control – it is not acceptable to instruct someone else to place the mics for you, or to adjust the placement once you have set them up.
2. You must set all the levels for the input process yourself.
3. Any settings on the recording device, including muting/arming tracks must be under your direct control.
4. Your recording must stay on the school/college premises at all times (you can't take it home or access it from home). You may however mix it down to a finalised CD (in a format such that you could not do any further work on it outside of school/college) so that you can listen to the mix in a number of different environments. Your teacher **must** be aware of this happening and take appropriate steps to ensure that controlled conditions remain in place. Be extremely careful about taking any of your practical work outside of your centre – always check with your teacher first, because the consequences of doing this without permission are likely to be severe.
5. Any preparation work you bring into school/college must be checked by your teacher/supervisor before you restart 'writing time'.
6. You can access the internet during your preparation time, but not during the recording process.

7. You must complete all aspects of the recording, from the first take to the final mix within 20 hours (this does not include any preparation time).

In addition to completing your work under controlled conditions, there are some other considerations to ensure that you meet the specification requirements:

- Length of recording
- Track count
- Minimum number of tracks captured using microphones
- Using overdub recording techniques
- Using only live musicians.

Length of recording

The final mix should last no less than two minutes and no longer than four minutes. It is perfectly acceptable to alter the structure of your chosen song to fit within this timeframe by, for example, dropping a verse and chorus.

Track count

There must be a minimum of eight tracks in your recording. This does not necessarily mean that you need eight different instruments – you can generally calculate how many tracks there are by counting the number of mics you have used to capture the sound source.

The specification states that there should be a maximum of 12 tracks used, but you will not be penalised if you use more than 12 tracks in your recording. However, be aware that the maximum was put in as a guide to try and encourage quality rather than quantity. If you go way above the maximum track count and the mix is overly busy and muddy, your marks will suffer.

If you intend to record a drum kit and want to use an eight-mic setup then you will almost certainly go over the maximum track count, but an examiner would prefer a piece with 15 tracks including a well recorded drum kit, with all the elements of the kit clearly defined, than one in which the snare is lost and the crash cymbal dominates just because you didn't feel you could use any more mics to keep within the track count.

Note that it is not necessary to record a drum kit in order to reach the minimum track count. Many students opt to avoid this very challenging task at AS level, deciding to concentrate on honing their mic placement skills on more straightforward instruments in the first year of the course. Again, an examiner is interested in the quality of capture across the whole recording and is not concerned about what instruments are used, even if you have decided to change the instrumental combination from what was used on the original, professional recording (see later for more detail on song choice and instrumentation).

Minimum number of tracks captured using microphones

A minimum of four tracks should be captured using microphones, no matter what the final track count is. It is acceptable to use DI recording techniques where you feel it is appropriate (such as when recording bass guitar or synths), but you must use mics for at least four of the tracks in your recording.

You do not have to use DI recording techniques if you do not feel it is appropriate for the instrumental combination you are using. The specification states that the recording should 'contain a balanced use of close-mic and direct-inject (DI) capture', but in some instances a balanced use will mean that no DI capture is used at all (such as with an ensemble consisting of vocals, acoustic guitars, percussion and piano). It is unacceptable to **only** use DI capture – a minimum of four tracks must be captured using microphones.

Using overdub recording techniques

The recording must make some use of overdubbing – it is not acceptable to capture the whole recording in one live take. It is acceptable to capture multiple instruments in one live take (such as the rhythm section), but you must overdub at least one more track afterwards.

Use of MIDI and loops or samples is prohibited in this task – you must only use live musicians.

How can I best use my time to complete the task?

Plan your time carefully!

The majority of time you spend should be in preparation, so that the actual completion of the task within the allotted 20 hours runs smoothly. It has been said that recording studios are the most expensive rehearsal rooms available – do not let this happen to you. Be aware that your school or college will have a procedure in place for booking studio time and rehearsal rooms and that, if you have one studio for the whole centre, other students will be jostling for use of the same space.

The following is a list of points you need to consider before you enter the studio:

- Choosing music to record
- Researching the style
- Rehearsing the musicians
- Planning the recording session
- Checking equipment
- Selecting recording space and preparing acoustics.

All these points fall under 'preparation time', so you can take as much time as you need to achieve the best possible results. Time spent preparing will pay dividends in the long run. Do not short-change yourself with insufficient preparation for this task.

How can I make best use of the equipment available to me?

It is possible to obtain a near-professional level recording from inexpensive equipment nowadays. The main ingredient for success is attention to detail. If you take care with the little things, making sure each stage of the process is as good as it can be, it is possible to achieve great results, no matter what equipment is available. However, it is important to have a decent selection of microphones from the outset (although they do not have to be too expensive).

As with the sequencing task, it is important to play to the strengths of the equipment you have available. For example, if you know that you do not have a good mic for recording a kick drum or bass guitar, then avoid choosing a stimulus that requires you to record a kick drum and DI the bass guitar. Similarly, if you have an excellent mic for recording strings and a good venue in which to record them, you may wish to include these in your recording.

Learn how to use each piece of equipment to the maximum of its potential. Read the following pages on microphone placement and use of effects and learn how to apply these techniques to the equipment you have available.

Remember: if you let little, seemingly insignificant mistakes pile up they will eventually become very significant – pay attention to detail!

Completing the recording task

○ Preparation – stimulus choice, researching the style, rehearsing, session planning, checking equipment, considering acoustics and setting up
○ Capture – sound, polar patterns, microphone types and microphone techniques
○ Editing – processors and effects
○ Mixing
○ Completing the logbook.

Preparation

Stimulus choice

As with most tasks, the most important thing to consider is the choice of stimulus material. For the sequencing and arranging tasks Edexcel has chosen the stimulus material for you. When the examiners considered the stimulus material for these tasks, they spent a considerable amount of time researching various options and ruling out unsuitable choices for a variety of reasons. They did not simply pick something they liked on a whim – they picked material that would allow an able and hard working student to score full marks. You should go through a similar thought process.

The music you choose to record must be a piece of music that is commercially available – one that you can go out and buy on CD or download from a commercial music site. It is not acceptable to record a song by your own band, even if you have released it commercially.

Will the choice of material allow you to get into the top bracket of each area of the mark scheme? It is unwise to choose a song that is deliberately lo-fi or makes use of clipping or noise in its production – this might not do so well in the 'noise and distortion' criterion. How is an examiner to differentiate between what clipping is deliberate and what is not?

What performers are available? In particular, have you chosen a song that you can get someone to sing successfully? Often a well-recorded track has been ruined by a poor vocal performance. It is acceptable to make an arrangement of a song to suit the performers you have available – you do not have to include all the parts that are in the original recording. This does not mean that you should deliberately do a completely different version (such as a reggae version of a rock classic), but the instrumentation can be altered to suit circumstances. It is also acceptable to alter the song structure to fit within the 2–4 minute time restriction. Ensure that all the important sections of the song are included (intro, verse, chorus, bridge, solos, outro), but you may wish to cut down a solo, drop a verse and chorus, shorten an intro, fade out a long outro and so on. Check that the music fulfils the track count requirements and change the arrangement if required.

Researching the style

Unlike the sequencing task, it is not a requirement of the multi-track recording task to reproduce an exact copy of the stimulus material, but you can aim for this if you wish. One benefit of this approach is that you do not have to 'reinvent the wheel' – you do not have to decide on what effects and processors you should use for each of the tracks from scratch, you can just copy what you hear on the stimulus track. However, if you are going to make an arrangement of the original stimulus material by altering the instrumentation in some way then the original approach to processing and mixing may not work for the new version, so you will have to reselect appropriate effects and processors. It would be possible to process and mix the recording by experimenting with various effects and processors, going through all the presets, editing the parameters and deciding on what might work best with your recorded audio, but this is a long and laborious process for which you may not have time.

The most time efficient approach is as follows:

1. Listen carefully to the stimulus track as if you were cloning it, and list the tracks and any production techniques you can hear, including the relative levels of different instruments and their position in the stereo field.
2. List the effects and processors you can hear on each track.
3. Annotate the list by adding any effects parameters you can hear on each track (e.g. Backing vox – long, dark reverb, high wet ratio).
4. Listen to other songs **in the style of your own arrangement**. If your recording is going to be in the same style as the original then this will not be so important, because you can just copy the

Remember: this is a recording task, not an arranging task. You will receive no credit for any arrangement techniques you use and will in fact be wasting your valuable time doing this unnecessarily. You should only differ from the original recording if you have a valid logistical reason for doing so. You should not change anything just for the sake of it.

original, but if you are forced into changing the style because of the instrumental forces used, you may need to listen to other music. Again, list the effects and parameters for other songs in this style.

5. Using audio material **that is not for your final recording**, experiment with the effects units and processors at your disposal (these may be hardware, stand-alone units or plugins incorporated into your audio sequencing package), trying to find similar sounds to those used on the material you researched in points 2–4. Either save these user settings or write them down in a logbook for later use with your recorded task material.

Rehearsing

Ensure that the musicians all have a copy of the stimulus material and clear instructions on what you want to do with it (i.e. either tell them to copy the CD exactly, in every possible detail or list any changes you want to make to structure, instrumentation or style). It would also be a good idea to double check with the musicians themselves that they are capable of performing the track, especially the vocalists – it may be the case that you think a singer is capable of performing a certain track in the given key, but they do not feel that they can (in which case you will either have to change the key or find a different song to record).

Check the availability of the musicians and plan a rehearsal schedule, which you should also attend. By the way, it is worth pointing out at this stage that it is not a good idea for you to record yourself performing, so recording your own band is a bad idea – it makes life much more complicated if you have to set up all the recording equipment, check levels etc. **and** perform the part. Some people can do this successfully, but it is not to be recommended.

During rehearsals you are acting as a producer – you should make decisions according to the production values you have researched. This will include discussing with the musicians what synth and guitar sounds you think are appropriate, checking the EQ and level of compression on the bass amp and what type of cymbals the drummer is using. Remember that the musicians are doing you a favour, so treat them with respect, making any suggestions that they change any aspects of their sound or performance in a way that will not offend them.

If you plan to use a guide track for the recording you need to ensure that the drummer can play along to a click and practise doing so.

Are the musicians used to playing with headphones? If not, they need to practise doing so, especially singers who may struggle with their tuning if they are not used to wearing headphones and drummers who may encounter problems with their volume levels because they aren't getting the natural acoustic feedback they are so used to. Ask what each musician's monitoring requirements are and set up a basic monitor mix. Note down your settings.

As you come close to being happy with the preparation of the raw materials, it is time to think about booking in some recording sessions.

Session planning

Set aside a suitable amount of time to record all the live audio you need to capture. Book in recording slots that fit with your musicians' schedules with a little extra time to allow for inevitable problems.

The order of recording tracks is important to get right. You will have discussed with the musicians the way they prefer to work (for example, drums and bass, then guitars, then vocals), so you will need to ensure that this is possible with the stimulus you have selected. For example, if the main guitar riff comes in before the rest of the band, you will need to have some way of counting in the guitarist (continuing the count until the rest of the musicians come in) or else you will struggle to get the timing right when you record the drum track first and there is no time reference for the guitarist to follow when he comes to do his part.

Ensure that you have all the appropriate information regarding monitor mixes and that you know how to set these up using the available equipment. Practise doing this before you go into the recording session.

Checking equipment

Check that all leads are fully functional and crackle free. Check that all input and output sockets on guitars, synths, basses and amps are in good working order. Check that the recording gear you will be using is (a) available for your session and (b) currently working. Check with the musicians about the state of their strings/reeds/throats. Make sure all instruments are in tune with themselves and each other (or the previously recorded tracks). Check the intonation setup on the guitars. Ask your music teacher to book in a piano tuner if you are recording a school piano. Check the drum kit for rattles and squeaks (including the drum stool). Check the quality of the drum skins and cymbals (especially the cymbals). If the basic sound of the cymbals is poor there is little you will be able to do later to fix this, so it is worth investigating borrowing good quality cymbals from someone (or don't record drums). Tune the kit and experiment with dampening (more on this in Unit 3).

Considering acoustics

The space in which you record has a significant impact on the sound you will capture. Later we will be looking at microphone placement, including stereo mic techniques in which the acoustics of a recording space are of paramount importance. If you are planning on using room mics of any sort or are micing from a distance, it is important to consider whether the sound of the room will have a detrimental effect on your final product. The live room/vocal booth may already have some acoustic treatment, and you may feel that it is suitable for some instruments but not for others. If you are recording vocals you will want to capture as much of the direct vocal sound and as little of any external ambience as is possible, so you may need to add additional dampening to the walls. Check the 'Studio SOS' articles in the excellent monthly recording magazine, 'Sound on Sound' for some tips on DIY acoustic treatment (generally involving hanging duvets around the recording space). They deal with many different environments and past articles are available online at **www.soundonsound.com**. If you try to add reverb to a track that already has natural reverb due to its recording environment, some unpleasant sonic artefacts may appear. You will need to address this issue, as you will not get any marks for stating in the recording log 'the reason my vocal track sounded bad was….'

When considering the recording environment, listen carefully (while everything is silent) for any noise. Listen for the hum from lights, the whirring of a computer fan, noise from an air conditioning unit, traffic noise, voices from a class next door or the noise of students running down the corridor. If any of these exist, try to plan ways of either eliminating them altogether or of minimising the impact on the quality of your recording.

Setting up

You have completed the preparation stages described above, have booked your studio time and are now ready to record! The next stage is to set up all the microphones and check levels. This is a stage that falls somewhere in between preparation and writing time. It is still, officially, preparation, but it has to be supervised by your teacher so that the authentication statement can be signed at the end of the process.

The next section goes into some detail about the use of various microphones and their different characteristics. Make sure you have read, understood and have practised these techniques to some extent before you go into the studio for your proper recording project so that, when you now enter the studio it is just a case of putting into action what you already know.

Capture

To successfully capture audio it is important to recognise the characteristics of the instrument (or voice) to be recorded – i.e. where the sound is generated, how it is amplified and any inherent problems associated with recording this instrument. When you know what it is that you are trying to capture then you can set an appropriate trap – the correct choice of microphone – in the appropriate place.

Sound

Sound is created when an object vibrates, causing tiny changes in the air pressure around it, creating a sound-pressure wave. The sound-pressure waves flow from the point where the sound was generated, through the air (as an expanding sphere), gradually diminishing until they are no longer perceptible. The frequency of waves is measured in Hertz (Hz), where 1 Hz is one cycle per second. The generally accepted range of human hearing is 20 Hz–20 kHz (kiloHertz), so the original object must be vibrating between 20–20,000 times per second in order for it to be audible to the human ear. As humans get older, their hearing deteriorates so that the frequencies at the extremes (particularly the high end) are no longer audible. This is why children can often hear some high-pitched sounds that are imperceptible to adults. Hearing can also be damaged by excessive exposure to loud noise, reducing the audible frequency range.

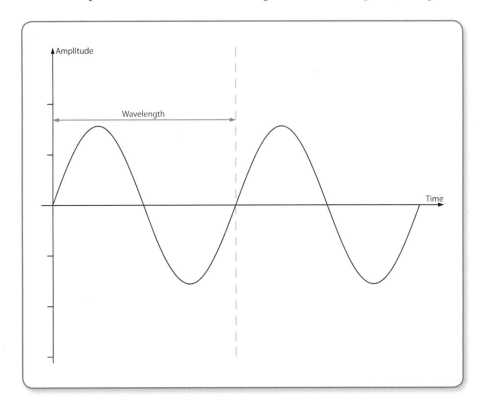

In addition to **frequency** a sound-pressure wave has an **amplitude** which we hear as volume and a **wavelength** which we do not actually perceive, but which has implications when it comes to microphone placement.

Polar patterns

Depending on how they have been built, microphones will pick up sound in different ways and from different directions. The directional characteristics of a microphone (i.e. which way you have to point it to capture a sound) are known as its **polar pattern**.

There are three main polar patterns – omnidirectional, cardioid (or unidirectional) and figure-of-eight.

Omnidirectional

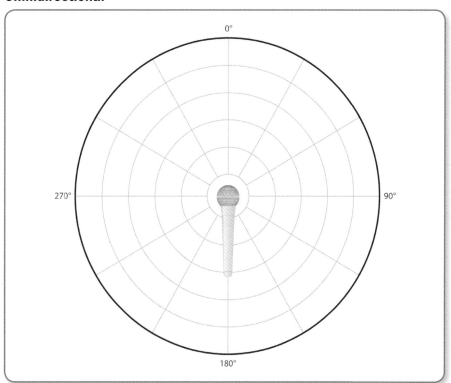

Cardioid

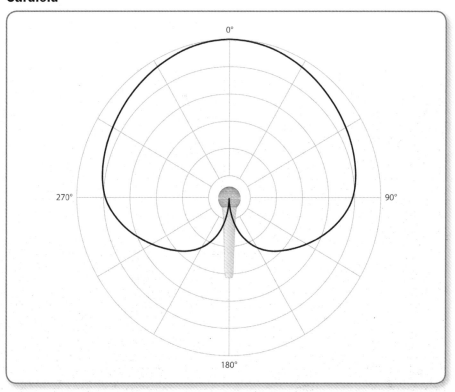

Figure-of-eight

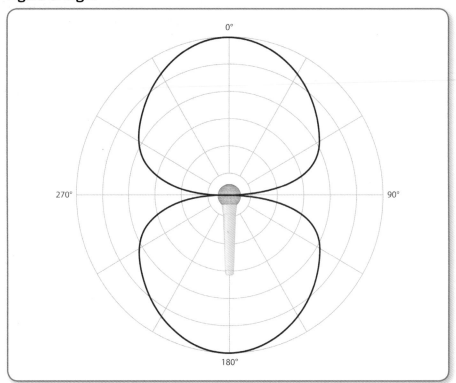

Omnidirectional microphones pick up sound evenly from any direction. In theory, there will be a slight obstruction caused by the physical body of the microphone itself, but it is not really important to consider this when using an omnidirectional mic. It is important to remember that although most polar pattern diagrams are represented in two dimensions (as in the examples above), the sound is picked up in three dimensions, so imagine the omnidirectional pattern to be a big sphere with the mic body at the centre of the sphere.

Cardioid microphones are also known as unidirectional microphones, because they pick up sound better from one direction than from any other. The pattern, when represented in two dimensions, looks a bit like a heart shape, hence the name 'cardioid'. The body of the mic is generally the 'null' point of the polar pattern, so cardioid mics (such as a Shure SM58) do not pick up sound coming from directly behind. This would be very useful when recording a drum kit – if the snare mic is positioned so that the back of the mic points towards the hi-hat then the snare mic will pick up the minimum of spill from the hi-hat. It is important to note that a cardioid polar pattern picks up sound from the sides of the mic almost as well as it does sound from the front. The extent to which it rejects sound from the side is determined by how directional it is.

Figure-of-eight microphones pick up sound evenly from the front and the back, but completely reject sound from the sides. This can be very useful in certain mic techniques when complete rejection of sound from one direction is required. Figure-of-eight mics are often used in conjunction with other mics to create a clear stereo image in ambient stereo recording.

Another common polar pattern, which is a refinement of the main three patterns is known as hypercardioid.

Hypercardioid

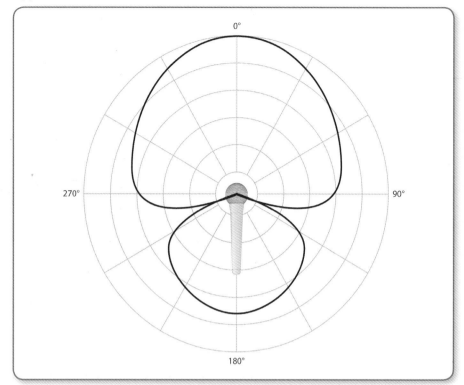

Hypercardioid mics combine elements of the cardioid and the figure-of-eight patterns – they are more directional than cardioid mics i.e. they pick up less sound from the sides, but they also pick up a little sound from behind the mic.

Microphone types

Polar pattern characteristics are often dependent on the design of the mic and how it has been manufactured. Since a microphone basically picks up the changes in air pressure, there are many ways it can do this. Some ways require a very sensitive, delicate design which will probably be more accurate in what it picks up, but much more susceptible to damage. More robust designs will have their limitations in what they can pick up. So all microphone design is a compromise between the quality of the audio capture and the necessity of making a practical device that can withstand the rigours of everyday use.

The standard types of microphone are:

- Dynamic
- Condenser
- Back-electret
- Boundary
- Ribbon
- Contact.

Dynamic microphones

The robust working mic for many stage vocalists is commonly a dynamic microphone. The construction of a dynamic mic means that it is more hardy than some of the other mic designs and, in some cases, can be dropped without any ill effects. This is quite an important design feature for live work. The manufacturing process is generally quite straightforward due to the simplicity of the design so, along with the economy of scale, this keeps the cost of dynamic mics quite low.

Dynamic microphones are also able to cope with high sound pressure levels (SPLs) without any concern for their wellbeing. They are thus useful for very loud instruments that might damage a more delicate mic.

Common dynamic microphone

The main drawback of a dynamic microphone is that it does not respond terribly well above approximately 16 kHz (depending on the make and model), so it is not as good as some other designs at capturing high frequency sounds. It will often have a slightly uneven response across the frequency range (some mics have become famous due to the subjectively pleasing nature of their uneven frequency response). Dynamic mics are good at capturing sound sources that are close to the mic, but not so good at picking up sounds that are further away – they produce a relatively small signal that needs a lot of amplification before it can be heard so, since distant sounds need even more amplification, they tend to get a little lost in the general background electronic noise. Thus, dynamic mics are generally poor choices for stereo ambient recording or for using as a distant pair, but they are perfect choices for a drum kit, guitar amp or a rock vocalist, certainly in a live setting.

Most readily available dynamic mics have a cardioid polar pattern, but some mics designed for a particular purpose (such as clip-on drum mics) are available as hypercardioid. Omnidirectional dynamic mics are also available, but they are slightly rarer.

Condenser microphones

Also known as capacitor microphones, condensers are the standard studio microphone. They work on a different principle to dynamic mics, requiring a power source to charge up the diaphragm inside the microphone. This is normally supplied from a source called **phantom power** that provides a 48V power supply to the microphone along the mic lead.

A condenser microphone in a shockmount

Condenser mics are a more complicated design, requiring intricate manufacturing processes, so they tend to be more expensive than their dynamic counterparts. They are much more sensitive at high frequencies than dynamic mics and are therefore suitable for recording any instruments that have high-frequency content including acoustic guitars, strings and cymbals. In fact, they can be made to have a fairly even response from below 20 Hz to well above 20 kHz, making them very useful for many applications. They also respond very well to low level signals and can successfully capture more distant sound sources making them much more suitable to stereo ambient recording than dynamic mics.

Condenser mics are more delicate than dynamics, making them susceptible to damage. They are much more likely to be irreparably damaged by a fall, so care needs to be taken when using and transporting them than is the case with dynamic mics. There have been some design changes over the last couple of decades allowing more robust models to be made for live work, with some artists taking these on because of the increased high-frequency response and more true-to-life response across the whole frequency range (with less peaks at different points in the mid-range). However, the added high-frequency response itself can add problems in a live context because it is more likely to cause feedback issues.

Condenser mics are available in any polar pattern with some containing two or more diaphragms, allowing the user to switch between different polar patterns.

Back-electret microphones

Essentially a cheaper version of a condenser mic, back-electrets use a slightly different manufacturing process allowing a battery to be installed in the body of the mic to provide the charge required to operate the microphone. Most back-electrets can also use phantom power (which will generally deliver a better sound quality than battery). Other than the ability to combine multiple diaphragms into one mic, which they lack, they possess many of the characteristics (positive and negative) of a condenser.

Boundary microphones

Pressure zone microphones (PZMs) are commonly used in schools as an easy way to pick up a wide sound field without having to be too careful with mic placement. They manage this by capturing the reflected sound off a large, solid surface (such as a floor or a wall) and are known as 'boundary mics' because they need to be positioned on a boundary in order to function properly. Boundary mics are omnidirectional (hence their ability to pick up a wide sound field). They can be useful for capturing the general room sound and adding some of this into the mix. They are also useful for ambient recordings, particularly in conjunction with a pair of condenser omnidirectionals or cardioids.

Ribbon microphones

Ribbon microphones have long been a favourite of orchestral sound recordists because of their ability to impart a certain warmth to a recording while still managing to capture the full frequency range very accurately. They are particularly prized for recording string sections. They work on the same principle as dynamic microphones, generating a very small electrical charge by the movement of the diaphragm (in this case, the ribbon), but they are amplified at source by a transformer designed specifically for the microphone. Until relatively recently they were exceedingly delicate, but modern production techniques have made them easier to transport and more affordable.

Contact microphones

Contact microphones pick up sound by being in direct contact with the sound source to be amplified. One of the most popular forms of contact mic would be the piezo crystal pickups used in acoustic guitars. These pickups generate an electrical charge when they sense any movement on the surface to which they are attached. Contact mics are particularly useful in situations where there is a high risk of feedback if one of the other microphone types were to be used. The main drawback of contact mics is that the frequency range is not faithfully reproduced – there is significant coloration introduced to the sound.

Microphone techniques

Microphone placement

The general rule of microphone placement is to experiment. The following ideas are just starting points – what will work for you will depend on the quality of the instruments you are recording, the room size and acoustics, the microphone types, the style of music and the performers themselves. None of the following are hard and fast rules. Don't just set the mics up as illustrated here and expect to get a great sound straight away – experiment, experiment, experiment!

Recording a vocal

When vocalists sing, there is a tendency for the plosive sounds (b's and p's) to cause a popping sound because a rush of air hits the diaphragm of the microphone. To avoid this, a mesh of material will break up the rush of air, but still let the microphone pick up the wanted sound. A convenient solution is to use a pop shield that can be attached to the mic stand and placed between the performer and the mic. You may wish to use a second mic stand for the pop shield if it is awkward to fit alongside a mic cradle.

In a studio situation, a condenser mic is the usual choice for recording vocals because of the flat frequency response and the high frequency sensitivity. For live work a dynamic mic can be used. Some vocalists will choose to use a dynamic mic because the mid-range hump in the frequency response actually suits their vocal style, making it sound more powerful. However, a condenser mic is the standard choice. The vocalist should stand between 15–45 cms away from the mic, with the mic a little above or below the mouth (not directly in front to avoid excess plosives). The normal choice of polar pattern for this setup is cardioid, although an omnidirectional mic may give a more natural response in some instances (if the acoustics of the room are acceptable).

Note: the vocalist should not hold the mic – when they move their hands, low frequency rumble will be transmitted down the mic cable. Ideally, a condenser mic should be placed in a sprung mic cradle (like that in the diagram) so as to avoid picking up any rumble from direct contact with the floor (via the mic stand). This is also known as a 'shockmount'.

Consider the acoustics of the position in which the singer is standing. Dampen the surrounding walls or hang dampening material around the vocalist if appropriate.

Recording acoustic guitar

The simplest way to record an acoustic guitar is that shown in the diagram:

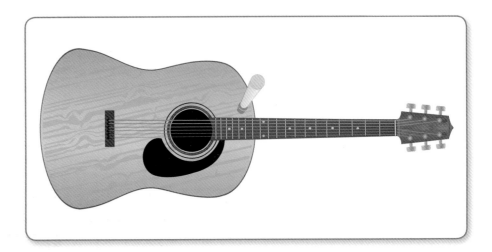

The advantage of using one microphone is that there will be no additional problems when it comes to combining two separate signals at the mixing stage. The disadvantage is that you are focussing on the sound coming from just one part of the guitar, whereas in real life you hear the sound from the guitar as a whole. If you choose to use a two mic setup, you may want to consider setting them up at more of a distance as a stereo pair, almost as an ambient recording. In either case, single mic or multi-mic setup, you should use condensers.

An omnidirectional pattern will pick up a more natural sound, but will equally pick up the sound of the room, while a cardioid pattern will depend much more on exactly where you point it, but will reject much of the background noise. Point the mic somewhere near where the neck joins the body, about 20cm or more away from the performer. Experiment with moving the mic slightly closer to the soundhole or further up the neck to get the right balance of direct sound, pick noise and finger-scrape. If the mic is positioned directly over the soundhole it will be too boomy. If the mic is positioned beyond the bridge of the guitar it will sound too nasal.

Recording electric guitar

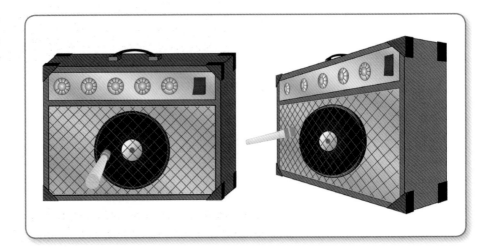

When using one mic for a guitar cab, it is generally best to position it as close as possible to the speaker grille, pointing slightly towards the centre of the cone from just inside the cone's perimeter. Be careful that the bass frequencies are not accentuated by the proximity effect if you get too close though.

If you are using an open-back cab you may wish to experiment with a mic at the back of the cab instead of/as well as in front, or a mic some distance away from the cab to capture the room sound. For close-mic applications you can use either a condenser or a dynamic mic, depending on whether your condenser mics are happy with high SPLs or not. If you use a mic in front and back of the cab, experiment with the phase button to see if it makes any difference to the sound.

The cab may need to be taken off the ground to avoid transferring vibrations through the floor to the mic instead of through the air – set it on some acoustic foam for this purpose.

Some guitarists will prefer to use an amp modelling device to record. These are very useful in that you do not have to worry about any spill onto the guitar track from the monitor and the sound will have a certain amount of processing on it by default, so it may sit in the mix a little bit easier. Other guitarists will swear by the direct amp sound and swear at you if you make them use an amp modelling device!

Recording upright piano

Before you start to record any piano in a school setting, try to get it tuned and checked for rattles and buzzes. Oil the pedals and select a stool that doesn't squeak.

The simplest way to record an upright piano is to place a spaced pair, about three octaves or so apart, facing slightly inwards towards the centre of the strings, with the front of the mics just inside the lid. They should not be pointing directly at the hammers or you may pick up too much of the percussive hammer noise as they strike the strings. If you feel this sound is too immediate, you may want to back them off a little. Condenser mics will be best for this job – use a matching pair.

Editing

After the source sounds have been successfully captured – and you do need to ensure that you are happy with the quality of the source sounds – it is time to edit the tracks.

As modern recording technology progresses, there is ongoing development of new and more powerful sound-sculpting tools. It is now possible, with the right tools, to make a silk purse from a sow's ear, but this is not advisable. The gift of alchemy does not come without a price – in this case it is the monetary price of the right equipment and programs but also, more importantly, that of time. You have 20 hours in which to complete the recording task, so this time is better spent ensuring that the initial sound capture is accurate than trying to tidy up poor timing in the bass guitar part by editing the audio afterwards.

How much basic sound editing you can do depends on the recording medium you have used. In the days of 8-track tape, very little editing was possible on the actual recording medium. In the heady days of digital audio workstations (DAWs), it is possible to cut, paste, splice and generally manipulate the original audio beyond recognition. If you use a standalone hard disk recorder, this editing will not be quite so easy as on a DAW, but it is still possible to some extent.

Before you begin to apply effects and processors it is important to tidy up the recorded audio as much as possible – this involves cutting any untidy beginnings and endings off takes, deciding between various takes as to which one you are going to use and compiling multiple takes into one 'comp-track' where the best sections of each performance come together to form one track, disregarding the unused material. You should eliminate any unwanted 'silences' and ensure that the signal level is consistent across the length of each track. This may require some normalising of audio and some editing of gain levels for individual sections.

Ensure that at this stage (if not before), you label all the tracks appropriately so that they are recognisable at a glance. Most DAWs will let you colour-code tracks for instant identification. This is a useful tool, but do not allow it to side-track you for long from the real task – pretty colours are all very well, but you can't hear them on the final mix!

Processors and effects

For the purposes of clarity, we shall use Paul White's (editor of Sound on Sound) definition of processors and effects – a processor is something which is applied to the whole signal and an effect is something which is applied to part of the signal only. This is a general rule of thumb, but is a good distinction to make. Processors will therefore include EQ, compression, limiter and gate while effects will include reverb, delay and modulation effects (such as chorus and flanger). You will have experimented with the effects units available to you during the preparation stage of the multi-track recording, and should have noted any settings from your stimulus audio that you wish to emulate or any production techniques you have noted from the stimulus style you researched earlier. You should also have saved some settings that you can now apply to the recorded audio. Note that compression settings will always need some considerable adjustment in order to be successful with a different track. Take some time to experiment with compression on the tracks that require it. Compression is examined under the 'management of dynamics' section of the mark scheme. If any tracks feel like they have variable dynamics over the course of the recording you must adjust them accordingly, either by checking that the gain settings are the same through each section of the song or by applying appropriate (and judicious) compression to help them sit well with the other tracks. EQ will also need very individual adjustment for each track.

It is often a good idea to save different versions of your track before you do any wholesale editing. This means that if you apply quite a lot of changes to your recording which you later want to undo you can instantly go back to a previous version.

> The golden rule when applying processors and effects is: Frequently compare the processed track with the unprocessed track. Does it sound better? If not, start again.

Mixing

You should leave some time between the previous stages and the mixing stage to allow your ears to freshen up. You have become very used to certain sounds, and probably immune to certain frequency issues in some of the tracks. When you come back to the recording with fresh ears you will instantly spot things you just couldn't hear before. At some point during this process most producers/engineers get the horrible feeling – 'what on earth was I thinking when I did that?!' Do not panic when this happens. It is natural to become deaf to certain aspects of a mix when you have been listening to it for many hours. It is much better that you discover errors within the 20 hours' time limit, and then correct any mistakes, than to let the examiner discover them after submission.

If you are trying to emulate a professional recording, frequently compare your mix to it. Refer to the notes you made during the preparation stage regarding the relative volume levels of the different parts. Remember that volume, panning and reverb are all interrelated – if you pan one backing vocal left and the other right, leaving the lead in the middle, it is less likely that they will be fighting for sonic space, and you are more likely to adjust the balance in an accurate way. Similarly, if a part is to sound further back in the mix, if you apply a fairly long reverb to it, it will sound further back.

A good way to think of a mix is to imagine a large room that you want to fill. The vertical plane is the frequency range with the floor at 20 Hz and the ceiling at 20 kHz. The depth of the room represents the amount and type of reverb you have applied with the dry sounds directly in front of you and the heavily reverberant sounds at the very back of the room. The width of the room represents the pan settings. The size of an object in the room represents its volume level. Have you filled the room without letting things overlap too much, and leaving some room to breathe? Are there big, yawning gaps in any place that need something to fill them? Hold this analogy lightly though, as it is more important to capture the nuances of the stimulus audio or style if it contravenes the principles above.

Completing the logbook

Questions 3–6 of the logbook refer to task 1B and ask for some details about the recording equipment used, the mic setup, recording procedure and details of EQ, FX etc. Fill this in as thoroughly as possible, listing every detail of the effort you have put into making your recording a success. If there is insufficient space on the track sheet, photocopy a blank track sheet, fill in the additional tracks and include it in the logbook. It may be more useful to attach photos for question 4 than to draw diagrams, so remember to bring a camera into the studio with you when you start setting up your mics.

As with the sequencing task, the only information the examiners have are the final audio track and your completed logbook. Make sure you let them know why they ought to be awarding you the marks.

What does the task entail?

This is the task where your creativity is really put to the test. The creative sequenced arrangement requires you to take an existing song and **develop** it into what is effectively a new piece in a new, **coherent** style. You will be able to choose between two stimuli released by Edexcel at the start of the AS year. You must develop the stimulus material so that it works within one of the two styles set by Edexcel. The stimulus songs and styles will change each year and do not necessarily link to the special focus styles in unit 2.

For this task there are two golden rules:

1. You must develop the given material. It is not enough to simply play through the material a couple of times and compose some interesting things around it. You must make creative use of the given material, but the original song should still be recognisable even after you have fully exercised your creative muscles.
2. The final arrangement must have a coherent sense of style throughout, including the most important ingredients or 'fingerprints' of the chosen style.

The printed stimulus material provided by Edexcel is a starting point for your arrangement. There may be other important elements of the stimulus song that have not been included in the printed material (e.g. if a chord sequence has been provided an important riff may not be notated, or an interesting intro omitted). It is perfectly acceptable to make use of this in addition to the printed material, but you must make some use of the printed material, treating it as the basis for your arrangement.

You do not need to produce a notated score for this task – all the marks are awarded on the basis of the final audio recording backed up by comments in the logbook.

What is the examiner looking for?

The examiner wants to hear a piece of music that contains the 'fingerprints' of the chosen stimulus style, is consistently within the boundaries of this style all the way through and makes extensive use of ideas taken from the original stimulus song. It is important that the examiner can tell, just by listening to the arrangement, what the stimulus song was, so the development of ideas should not be too convoluted and obscure so as to completely hide the identity of the stimulus. It is important to make use of the sequencing skills learned in task 1A to edit existing timbres and ensure that the final sequenced piece is musical with appropriate articulation, dynamics, panning and so on.

It is not necessary to develop every aspect of the stimulus material – it is possible to concentrate on three of the areas listed under the optional criteria in the mark scheme and gain maximum credit.

The mark scheme for task 1C differs from the mark scheme for tasks 1A and 1B in that not all of the criteria are used. The first three criteria are compulsory and are applied to every piece submitted, no matter what stimulus song or style is chosen. Examiners will mark all arrangements according to all five of the optional criteria and take forward the best three marks, ignoring the two weakest criteria.

Compulsory criteria (all assessed – 22 marks available):

1. Use of stimulus (6 marks)
2. Style/coherence (6 marks)
3. Use of Music Technology (10 marks)

Optional criteria (best three marks counted – 18 marks available):

4. Melody (6 marks)
5. Harmony (6 marks)
6. Rhythm (6 marks)
7. Texture and Instrumentation (6 marks)
8. Form/structure (6 marks)

The optional criteria of melody, harmony and rhythm are only used to assess ideas that you have come up with yourself (in addition to those given in the stimulus material) or that you have arrived at by significantly developing the original ideas in the stimulus material. In other words, you can't get credit for a great tune, chord sequence or groove that you have lifted directly from the stimulus song. However, if you have taken an idea and worked on it to make it your own in some way, you can still get credit.

1. Use of Stimulus

6	Ideas from the stimulus have been used imaginatively to create a very convincing piece of music. There may be new ideas introduced, but much of the material has been drawn from the stimulus itself and developed in a convincing way.
4 – 5	Ideas from the stimulus have been used to create a piece which may be a little predictable, but which works well. There may be some new ideas introduced, but most of the ideas are straightforward developments of material from the stimulus.
2 – 3	The stimulus material has been used with some development of the original ideas. There are some passages that do not work so well and there may be a significant proportion of the arrangement that simply states the original stimulus material rather than developing it.
1	The stimulus has either not been used much or has simply been repeated without any further development. There are many sections that do not work well. The arrangement may be shorter than two minutes.

2. Style/Coherence

6	The arrangement clearly displays the main elements of the chosen stimulus style. It is obvious what the chosen style is just from listening to the arrangement. The whole piece hangs together really well with a clear sense of direction (there are highs and lows in the piece and they feel as if they happen at the right time). All sections of the piece feel as if they really belong there.
4 – 5	The arrangement works in the chosen style, with elements of the style coming across clearly. The ideas work well together and there is enough variety in the piece to hold a listener's attention without feeling overly repetitive. If there are any sections that feel a little awkward, they still work to a certain extent.
2 – 3	There are some elements of the chosen style present in the arrangement, but the stimulus material doesn't always work in this style – there are a few uncomfortable moments. There is too much repetition or the ideas just seem to keep on happening one after the other without really linking together properly.
1	Few, if any, of the fingerprints of the chosen style are obvious to the listener. The different sections of the piece do not really hang together at all.

3. Use of Music Technology

10	The choice of sounds is appropriate to the chosen style and there has been some editing of presets. The parts have been programmed so that they sound musical – the articulation and phrasing make the parts sound like convincing musical performances. Dynamics have been shaped and the arrangement has been well balanced with appropriate panning.
8 – 9	The choice of sounds is appropriate to the chosen style. The parts have been edited to include some shaping of dynamics and some musical phrasing/articulation. The arrangement is well balanced with appropriate panning.
6 – 7	The choice of sounds works in context. There are dynamic contrasts, but no shaping. There is some musical articulation and phrasing, but not throughout, or it does not always work. The recording is mostly well balanced, but there are some parts that don't blend properly or can't be clearly heard. Panning is present, but may be slightly narrow.
4 – 5	Most of the sound choices are fine, but there is the odd poor choice. Some parts are lost in the mix or don't blend properly. The stereo field is used, but it may be too narrow or unrealistically wide. There are some general dynamic contrasts, but no shaping. There is some articulation and phrasing, but it sometimes sounds unmusical.
2 – 3	There are several poor choices of sound. Several parts are lost in the mix or leap out of the mix from time to time. There is little use of panning or it has been used inappropriately. There is a little articulation but, where it is used, it takes away from the arrangement rather than add to it. Any dynamic contrasts are extreme and unmusical.
1	Poor choice of sounds throughout. The balance is poor across the whole mix with no panning used at all. There are no dynamic contrasts or, where they are used, they are unmusical. There is no editing to try and make the phrasing sound musical.

4. Melody

6	The melodies work well within the chosen style – they sound stylish. They are imaginative and memorable. They have a good shape, flowing nicely (if appropriate to the style). Any new melodies compliment the existing material, not swamping it. If assessing melodies derived from the stimulus material: these have been reworked significantly forming new, but recognisable melodies, perhaps taking on a new character while retaining some recognisable aspects of the original.
4 – 5	Any new melodies work within the chosen style – they have some sense of shape. If assessing melodies derived from the stimulus material: any reworking of the melodies is successful, although they may not have changed their character significantly. Melodies from the original stimulus may have been used successfully in a different context.
2 – 3	There are some awkward points in the melodies – they do not always seem to flow or do not really reflect the chosen style. There may be some awkward intervals or they sound stilted. If assessing melodies derived from the stimulus material: there is some reworking of the original melodies, but this is either unsuccessful at times or else there are no recognisable elements of the stimulus melody left after having been reworked.
1	Melodies do not flow. They are not appropriate to the chosen style – they do not sound stylish at all. They are awkward and difficult to perform. If assessing melodies derived from the stimulus material: there are few changes from the original and, where these exist, they are unsuccessful.

5. Harmony

6	The chosen harmonies fit well within the chosen style. They do not clash with the melody in any way (unless clashes are clearly demanded by the style). There is an imaginative use of harmony, but in keeping with the style. The tonality of the arrangement is appropriate to the style. There is a successful reharmonising of the stimulus material.
4 – 5	The harmonies work throughout the piece, with perhaps the odd, insignificant clash. They are mostly stylish. The harmonies are not derived from the stimulus song – they are original and generally result in a successful reharmonising of the material. The tonality (including any key changes) is appropriate to the style.
2 – 3	There are some clashes in the harmony or the harmonies are dull and uninteresting. There has been some attempt made to reharmonise the stimulus within the chosen style, but there are some awkward moments where it doesn't quite fit.
1	The harmonies frequently clash with the melodic material. There has been little attempt to reharmonise the original, with any attempts proving unsuccessful.

6. Rhythm

6	The rhythm of the arrangement is completely in keeping with the chosen style so that it really captures the groove. Some of the rhythms from the stimulus song have been developed in an interesting and original way.
4 – 5	The rhythms used are appropriate to the chosen style. There is some development of some rhythmic features of the stimulus song.
2 – 3	The rhythms mostly work in the chosen style, but they may sound a little stiff or contrived. There is little development of rhythms from the stimulus song. The arrangement may have a boring, repetitive rhythm or far too many rhythmic ideas jostling for attention.
1	The rhythms do not really fit within the chosen style. There has been little or no development of the rhythms from the stimulus song.

7. Texture and Instrumentation

6	The choice of instruments is appropriate to the chosen style and may include some imaginative, but suitable additions. The choice of timbre for the lead part works with the other parts. The texture is interesting including contrasts appropriate to the chosen style.
4 – 5	The choice of instruments is mostly appropriate to the chosen style, although there may be one or two choices that don't sit quite so comfortably. The texture adds interest to the piece.
2 – 3	Some of the instrumental choices are not appropriate to the chosen style. The texture may remain too similar throughout or there may be some odd textural contrasts not in keeping with the chosen style.
1	There are many odd instrumental choices in the piece that do not work in the chosen style. There is no textural contrast or there are several serious misjudgements in the use of textural contrast.

8. Form/Structure

6	Uses the ideas from the stimulus and puts them into an interesting and coherent structure, different from the original. The structure is either something original or else it uses a structure typical of the chosen style, but does something imaginative with the stimulus material to make it work in a natural way.
4 – 5	The ideas have been organised in a way that suits the chosen stimulus style, possibly using a structure common to the stimulus style. The overall structure is coherent, working well although it lacks any real imaginative touches.
2 – 3	The musical ideas have been organised in a way that is overly repetitive or is too unpredictable. The structure may work in some ways, but is unsuitable for the chosen stimulus style, causing some awkward moments. There is little sense of direction in the structure.
1	The musical ideas have not been organised properly – there may be far too much repetition or a complete lack of direction.

What are the rules for completing the task?

The creative sequenced arrangement must be completed under controlled conditions.

For the creative sequenced arrangement, 'preparation time' will include the following:

- Learning and practising arrangement techniques
- Learning how to use the sequencing package
- Researching the stimulus songs – listening to the original songs and any available cover versions
- Researching the stimulus styles – listening to tracks by the suggested artists/bands
- Experimentation with the available sound sources to find timbres appropriate to the chosen style
- Finding samples as appropriate to the style
- Experimenting with the melodic, harmonic and rhythmic ideas in the chosen stimulus song
- Developing draft arrangement ideas for later input into the sequencer
- Annotating draft scores with new ideas and comments.

Any of the above may be undertaken in school/college or at home – it does not need to be directly supervised, but your teacher will need to regularly monitor your progress as you develop your arranging ideas.

When you do any work to the file that will eventually be mixed down into a stereo track for submission to the examiner it is considered 'writing time', so you must observe the following rules:

1. All work must be your own. The only exception is when you have used samples or loops that are acceptable as clearly stated on the front cover of the stimulus material (the details of what samples/loops are acceptable may change from year to year), in which case you must declare their use in the logbook.
2. You must complete all the input, editing and mixing of the arrangement under supervision by your teacher or another member of staff.
3. The sequenced file for your arrangement must stay on the school/college premises at all times (you can't take it home or access it from home), but you may print out a score and take this home for annotation.
4. Any preparation work you bring into school/college must be checked by your teacher/supervisor before you restart 'writing time'.
5. You can access the internet during your preparation time, but not during inputting, editing and mixing of your arrangement.
6. You must complete the input, editing and mixing of the arrangement within 20 hours (this does not include any preparation time).

You must ensure that the final stereo mixdown lasts between 2–3 minutes.

No live performances may be recorded for this task – it must all be sequenced.

How can I best use my time to complete the task?

Plan your time carefully!

This task requires an interesting combination of skills, particularly the creative skill of arranging a given idea, but also the practical skill of sequencing musical material. It is therefore strongly advised that you begin the sequencing task before you begin inputting your ideas for the arrangement. You will have built up a range of skills and time saving tricks having gained familiarity with the software and the equipment you are using. You will also have some idea of what can and cannot be achieved with the available kit. If you are working on several tasks at the same time then you should be researching the stimulus material and doing the preparation side of the arranging task while you learn the nuts and bolts of sequencing for task 1A.

There is probably a greater percentage of time that needs to be spent in preparation for this task than for tasks 1A or 1B. Developing musical ideas takes time, patience and discipline – it is not a good idea to imagine that you can sit down in front of a sequencing package and input your arrangement directly without having sweated the necessary blood beforehand! As such, it is unlikely that you will need all of the available 20 hours to actually input this task in 'writing time', but overall it will probably take longer than the other tasks.

Think ahead...

> ## Completing the arranging task
>
> O   Consider questions 9 and 10 of the logbook
> O   Research the chosen style
> O   Dissect the stimulus
> O   The tightrope.

There are 20 marks available for the logbook. These are all allocated to aspects of writing about your arrangement. If you incorporate this into your planning for the arrangement task then, not only will it make life much easier, it will probably help you to be more successful in both task 1C and the logbook.

How can I make best use of the equipment available to me?

Although the answer to this question is very similar to the answer given for the sequencing task (because of the obvious crossover in skills and use of equipment), there is an additional element to consider – when you are choosing the stimulus style for your arrangement, think carefully about whether the available equipment is suited to this style. For example, if one of the stimulus styles includes a significant proportion of distorted guitars and the other contains vintage analogue synth sounds, consider the strengths of the sound sources you have available before you decide to go down one route or the other. As with the sequencing task, playing to the strengths of the available equipment will make life much easier.

Unlike tasks 1A and 1B, the preparation element of arranging will continue alongside the writing (inputting) element. If you approach this task in the right way, preparation will take the vast majority of the time you spend on the task. It is possible that you will not use the full 20 hours for the actual writing time but, if you want to do the best you possibly can, you should schedule a lot more than 20 hours for research, preparation and development of ideas.

For some people, arranging may seem like a very daunting task. You may have some experience of songwriting in a band situation or of composing for GCSE Music, but arranging may be a whole new skill for you to learn. To be successful at this task it is important to approach it in a different way to composing. When you write a song or compose a piece from scratch, you probably start with an idea, be it a lyric, a concept, a melody, a riff, a groove, or even a particular sound, but when you start an arranging task, you already have a bank of materials to work with. When you compose, you have to decide on a style for your piece – probably something you are familiar with or something you are trying to create by combining various styles that have influenced you. However, for task 1C, you are given a choice of two styles within which to work, so you must observe the stylistic fingerprints that already exist. This may seem a bit restrictive at first but, as you immerse yourself in the task, you will discover that there are many creative decisions you have to make as you go along, and it is a great discipline to work within a set of boundaries. It is only possible to push boundaries if they exist in the first place!

The following is a suggested method of working in order to meet the requirements of this task. Even if you are a seasoned songwriter/composer, it is highly recommended that you at least consider the suggested steps so that you do not miss some aspect that is vital to success. Constantly refer to the paraphrased mark scheme given previously in this chapter and, as with the other tasks, be brutally honest in your self-assessment.

Consider questions 9 and 10 of the logbook

In the previous two tasks it was appropriate to complete the logbook at the end of the task, although you should have been keeping a record of various specific points as you went along. For this task it is better to consider questions 9 and 10 from the very beginning.

9 'Explain how you developed your creative sequenced arrangement from your chosen stimulus. Refer to at least two of the following: melody; harmony; rhythm; texture and instrumentation; form and structure.'

10 'Identify the most important features of your chosen style, and explain how you have used them in your arrangement.'

Approach these questions in reverse order. Firstly you should research the chosen style, listing all the features you possibly can and then include some of these in your arrangement. Secondly you should consider which of the optional criteria are most pertinent to your choice of style and decide how you may go about developing these aspects of the stimulus.

Research the chosen style

You should have already decided which of the two given styles is appropriate to use, considering the resources at your disposal and your own expertise. If not, now is the time to do so.

Along with the two stimulus styles, Edexcel has listed a number of artists/bands that are considered representative of each style. Gather as many albums/tracks as you can by each of the listed artists for your chosen style and listen to them, listing all the common musical features. You should listen for the following points, keeping a written record of your findings:

- Instrumentation
- Structure
- Texture
- Tonality
- Harmony
- Melody
- Tempo
- Rhythm/groove
- Mixing/production.

Even within any fairly well-defined style or genre there will be a range of responses for the above points (for example the quiet, slow ballads on the album will differ significantly to the upbeat songs), but if you study a number of artists, a pattern will emerge that helps to define the style. You may wish to differentiate between different types of song within the style and list the features separately for each type of track. You may wish to refer to the styles listed in unit 2 as a starting point for your research.

Instrumentation

Describe the instruments and instrumental combinations that are common to all, or most of the artists. Be as specific as possible when describing the sounds you can hear – don't just write 'vocals, electric guitar, bass, synth, drums', as this is too general and could refer to any number of styles – list the instruments you can hear and describe, in as much detail as possible, the timbre of each instrument. For example:

Instrument	Description
Vocals	Soulful female lead, three female backing singers in close harmony
Guitar	Clean, funky style electric guitar with compression
Bass	Mellow sounding electric bass. Very compressed and smooth
Synth	Washy string pads and occasional analogue lead – mostly sawtooth derived sound
Drums	Full kit. Lots of different cymbal sounds. Quite funky in places. Prominent snare. No percussion used.

Remember that this is a sequenced arrangement, so you have to think in terms of what timbres you have available that might best reproduce the sound of the chosen style. Consider the lead vocal sound in the same way as you did for task 1A – what timbre might best represent this in your arrangement?

As is the case for task 1A, for the top mark in the mark scheme (criterion 3 – use of music technology) you need to demonstrate some editing of timbres.

Structure

Any piece of tonal music (music that is in a key) can be broken down into sections, allowing for easier analysis. For example, a song generally has an introduction, verse, chorus, middle 8 (or bridge) and an outro (see the section on transcription for task 1A, page 13). Many songs also have solos and links between some sections (such as a pre-chorus). The first movement of many symphonies is often in sonata form. This has three major sections (exposition, development and recapitulation), each of which is broken down into smaller sections in which composers show their cleverness by developing their ideas in different ways, making use of lots of different keys. Instrumental rock music often uses a combination of ideas from the pop/rock world and from the world of classical music in order to organise the melodic and harmonic ideas.

Structure is determined by several aspects – in popular music a section tends to have a recognisable riff or chord sequence and a particular melody, both of which will return, perhaps in a slightly altered version, the next time the section occurs. The other sections will have different chord sequences and/or melodies to differentiate between them and to add interest. In classical music the key of a melody or harmonic pattern will also play a part in determining the structure.

The stimulus song will have a structure that you should become familiar with. Songs written in your chosen style may have a structure which differs little from band to band – artists often get into a formula of songwriting, so the structure of many of their songs can be quite similar.

Listen through three or four songs by each artist that you feel are typical of the chosen style. Write out the structures of each of these songs. Is there a pattern? If the majority of these songs follow a particular structure then you should use it as a basis for your arrangement – even better if it is a different structure to that of the stimulus song. Be aware that some artists deliberately set out to compose songs with complex and original structures that differ from song to song.

If you think that criterion 8: Form/structure may be one of the optional criteria used to assess your arrangement, you will need to think carefully about how original you can be within the chosen style – you do not want to do something that would never be heard in your chosen style, but neither do you want to slavishly copy something that has been done before. Remember that you can only get the full six marks if what you do is imaginative. Is there some way that you could use a simple, tried and tested structure, but also imaginatively use the ideas from the stimulus?

Texture

Texture is closely linked to instrumentation and structure. In a music technology sense, texture is determined by the production. Texture refers to the way instruments and sounds are brought in and out of the music and how they are combined at any given time. Some sounds contribute more towards thickening a texture than others simply because they are sustained timbres that cover a wide frequency range – a plucked string will contribute less to the density of the texture than a synth string pad. For example, a dense texture would be likely to have many instruments playing relatively busy parts at the same time. A sparse texture may have fewer parts – or it may still have many parts, but each playing far fewer notes, and not all playing at once. The texture will change as the song progresses, building up at certain points and thinning out at others to give the song a sense of light and shade.

The structure of the songs in your chosen style may be partially determined by the texture. For example, in many genres of dance music, there are one or more points in the song where there are breakdowns (dropping the texture down to perhaps just one part) followed by sections where the parts are gradually reintroduced to the texture. This breakdown-build up idea forms an important part of the structure of the song. In many songs, the texture in the chorus is fuller than that of the verse. Often the reason for this is that the lyrics in the verse are more complex than those in the chorus, so the producer is trying not to draw attention away from the vocal part. The hookline (the bit you will remember, normally kept simple so it will stick in your memory) is generally in the chorus, so there may be a big backing texture to support this, perhaps accompanied by a hook riff.

Listen again to the same songs you used to analyse the structure. Is there a common pattern for the texture in this style? List any points of interest you hear such as breakdowns, repeated choruses that build up the texture, sparse intros, dense instrumental bridges and so on.

To get full marks for this optional criterion you must use a selection of instruments that are appropriate to the chosen style. If you can add in a few extra elements for the 'ear candy' effect, confident that they add to the texture rather than detract from the coherence of the piece, then this will sound more imaginative. The texture will need to have contrast, adding interest to the arrangement. Contrasts will be partially determined by the structure, helping to add a sense of direction.

Tonality

A lot of chart music is in a major key, but there are styles (such as hip hop and metal) that make extensive use of minor keys. Styles that are influenced by world music will have drawn from the tonality of the region – for example, Celtic-influenced music may have a modal feel while Bhangra will contain an element of raga. Listen again to the songs by the artists in your chosen style and decide if they use more major keys than minor keys or vice versa. Also, listen to see if there are changes in tonality moving from section to section (especially moving into the bridge or instrumental).

In the mark scheme, the use of tonality as an arranging tool will be credited under optional criterion 5: harmony.

Harmony

Harmony is closely related to tonality, but focuses in on the individual chords and the relationship of the melody to the chords/riff.

One of the more recognisable elements of a style will be its use of harmony. This may not leap out at the listener as it is something you need to specifically listen for. Any style that uses extended chords (notes added to the basic triads to make them sound more exotic) will have a jazzy feel if it is a smoother, laid back style or a funky feel if it is more rhythmic. In some styles the harmonies are not really determined by chords, but rather by the overall sound of several melodies playing at once – for example, in a rock band where the singer is singing over a riff, there may be no instrument actually playing chords, but the combination of the parts at any given moment will still give an impression of harmony. Some styles will make extensive use of 7th chords, giving a bluesy feel. Others will use the occasional 'odd' chord to knock the listener off balance. Some styles have what is known as 'static' harmony, where the melodic parts may move over the top of a sustained/repeated chord or riff.

Listen for the following in your selection of songs from the chosen style:

1.   Is the harmony static or do the chords change frequently?
2.   How often do the chords change (once or twice per bar, once every two bars etc.)?
3.   Is there a chord sequence that appears commonly in songs by different artists within the style, or is there a restricted selection of chords that make up the chord sequences?
4.   Are the chords simplified (power chords – triads with the 3rd removed) or extended (additional 7ths, 9ths etc.)?
5.   Does the harmony differ from section to section?

To gain full marks for criterion 5: harmony, you will need to ensure that your chord sequences/riffs sound as if they belong in the chosen style – almost as if they have been written by one of the listed artists. It is probably better to start with imitation rather than trying to be overly imaginative and thus moving away from the chosen style in your quest for imagination and originality. The challenge is to try and be imaginative within the confines of the style. One way you could achieve this is to use the harmonic language of the chosen style, but to be clever in your approach to the way you move from section to section (another link to structure). Tonality is also assessed under this criterion – so imaginative key changes (as appropriate to the style) would help to add interest.

Melody

Analysing the melodic content of the stimulus style is a little more complex than some of the other elements, but is often the most immediately recognisable aspect of an artist's sound.

There are several areas to home in on when listening to the melodic content of a song:

1. The main vocal melody
   a. Is it melismatic or syllabic (are there several notes or just one note per syllable)?
   b. What is the tonality of the actual melody (which may be different to the overall tonality)? This may be pentatonic, major, minor, modal or monotone.
   c. Is the melody rhythmic and punchy or does it flow?
   d. How is the melody delivered by the vocalist? Does the vocalist swoop into and/or out of notes? Are there any tuning issues with the vocal delivery? Are there any points when the melody becomes semi-spoken?
   e. At what point in the bar do the phrases enter – do the vocal phrases always anticipate the bar, come in on the first beat or slightly after the start of the bar?
   f. Are the melodies angular (they leap about a lot) or do they generally move by step?
   g. What is the range of the melody – is it restricted or does it use the full vocal range?

2. The backing vocal parts
   a. How many backing vocal parts are there?
   b. Do they run parallel to the lead vocal (e.g. harmonising in thirds) or are they separate, interweaving melodies?
   c. How often do they come in? In which sections are they used?
   d. Listen also for the same points as listed for the main vocal melody.

3. Instrumental melodic lines
   a. Are there instrumental solos? Are there any noteworthy features in these solos?
   b. Are there countermelodies played by the instrumental backing – do they almost act as backing vocals from time to time?
   c. Is there a call and response texture between instruments or between an instrument and the main vocal line?

4. How the melody fits with the harmony
   a. Does the melody fit closely with the harmony or does it seem to deliberately work against the harmony from time to time, creating tension?
   b. Is it a pentatonic melody, disregarding the chord changes/riff underneath?

5. How does it differ from section to section?

It is important to have a grasp of how melodies work in the chosen style before trying to come up with new melodies or develop melodies from the stimulus. There will be a lot of potential melodic material ripe for development at your disposal in the stimulus song. If you can take these and manipulate them so that they sound at home in the chosen style then you are going in the right direction. Taking melodies from the stimulus song and using them out of context (such as using one as the basis for an instrumental solo or instrumental countermelody) is a rich resource to explore. As well as using the melodies in a different context, you should also **develop** the melodies.

To gain full marks for criterion 4: melody, the melodies will need to be imaginative and memorable, sounding as if they belong in the chosen style. The marks for this section will only be awarded to melodies that you have either come up with yourself or have significantly changed from the original stimulus song.

Tempo

The choice of tempo is not specifically assessed at any point, neither in the arrangement itself nor in the logbook. However, the choice of tempo will contribute to the groove and hence the marks for rhythm. The correct tempo will help to make an arrangement sound stylish. Try playing a familiar song too fast and it sounds rushed or even comedic, try playing it too slowly and it will sound dirge-like. As mentioned previously, it is unlikely that all the songs you are analysing will be at the same speed, but they are very likely to operate within a given range.

Rhythm/groove

For certain genres of dance music the rhythmic element defines the style. For some styles of music the rhythm is the driving force for the rest of the song and for others it is much less important. Identifying how prominent the rhythm section is in the mix and the role of rhythm/groove is an essential part of capturing the feel of the chosen style.

Listen to your song selection again, focussing on the following points:

1. Is the drum part programmed or played live?
2. Is additional percussion used (e.g. congas, cowbell, tambourine)? If so, identify the instruments.
3. What is the most common time signature used?
4. Is there a common, recognisable rhythm pattern (e.g. four-to-the-floor, straight rock rhythm, bossa nova)?
5. What beats do the kick and snare drum fall on?

6. How is the hi-hat used?
7. Are there any interesting syncopations or anticipations of the beat?
8. Does the groove feel edgy or laid-back?
9. How do the different elements of the rhythm section fit together (drums, percussion, bass, rhythm/acoustic guitar)?

Although the mark scheme states it will only award credit for rhythms that you have come up with, it would not be appropriate to create a completely new rhythm for your chosen style, especially if that particular rhythm defines the style – this would contradict other areas of the mark scheme! It is most important that you develop the stimulus song, using the rhythm/groove common to your chosen style. To gain the top mark in criterion 6: rhythm, you would need to make imaginative use of any rhythmic features you find in the stimulus song itself, not come up with new and imaginative ways of playing the rhythm from the chosen style.

Mixing/production

All of the above headings concentrate on traditional musical elements and how these have been used in the chosen style but, in recorded music, there is an additional element that can define style – the use of music technology.

In earlier recorded music such as early jazz and rock 'n' roll, the recordings are trying to capture a live performance as well as they can. There is little use of music technology in a creative sense (see the section in unit 4 for more details on the development of music technology, page 136). However, in modern music there has been an increasing reliance on music technology to record, edit, shape and otherwise manipulate the source sounds. The type of technology used can help define a style, even down to the use/abuse of a specific piece of kit (for example, the Roland TB-303 is 'the sound' of acid house music).

Listen to your selected tracks one more time, focussing on the mix and production techniques used. Listen for the following:

1. Recording quality – does the final recording sound old because of the crackling and generally poor quality? Is it digital or analogue?
2. Use of stereo field – is the recording mono/stereo/surround? Are there creative uses of panning in the production?
3. Is the production sparse, with care and attention to every detail of every timbre, or is it a wall of sound? This aspect is closely linked to texture.
4. Is the recording clean, pristine and polished or is it more lo-fi and raw?
5. Is there lots of 'ear candy' in the recording or do the production values lie in the way the live performances integrate with each other?
6. Use of processing – are any of the following present?
   a. Level of compression of individual tracks and the overall mix
   b. EQ – may be used in a creative way or to correct problems
   c. Gating
   d. Enhancer to add a shimmer to the high frequencies (related to EQ)
   e. Pitch correction (Autotune and related devices) – this may also be used in a creative way.

7. Use of effects
   a. Reverb types used (e.g. plate, spring, room, gated)
   b. Delay types used (e.g. slapback, thickening, echo)
   c. Modulation FX (e.g. chorus, flanger, phaser)
   d. Special FX (e.g. ring modulator, harmoniser, vocoder).

List all the important production aspects you can hear in the recording, but you need to bear in mind that you will be working in the MIDI domain, so try to think of ways to recreate these audio effects in the sequenced arrangement or some possible workarounds (you are not expected to faithfully duplicate any one recording, unlike in task 1A).

Dissect the stimulus

The stimulus song is a goldmine of musical ideas. You should not start the arranging task with your own musical ideas – instead you should carve the stimulus into chunks of musical raw material ripe for development.

- List the signposts
- Research covers and remixes
- Place the signposts in a new context.

List the signposts

Every famous song has at least one significant element that is instantly recognisable. We shall call this a 'signpost' – it points the way to the original song, no matter whether it has been taken completely out of context or not.

The stimulus songs will probably have several of these signposts, some more recognisable than others and some more useable than others for the purposes of the arranging task. Possible signposts will include:

1. A melody or melodic fragment – this may be as long as a whole phrase or as short as a few notes)

2. A chord sequence, chord change or even just one chord (e.g the chord from Stravinsky's 'Rite of Spring' is instantly identifiable).

3. A riff – may be a guitar, synth or bass riff, or a riff made up of parallel chords

4. A rhythmic feature (e.g. the drum beat of Queen's 'We Will Rock You' is instantly identifiable, well before the singing starts)

5. A particular sound – may be a sound effect or an instrumental timbre that immediately triggers the memory

6. A lyrical fragment.

Of these six possible signposts, numbers 1–4 can be used in many ways in your arrangement and can generally be moulded to fit into the stylistic elements you have researched in the previous section. Number 5 is a little tricky in this task – you should use recognisable timbres or sound effects taken from the stimulus song with care in your arrangement as they may not fit in the chosen style. If they do work then use them by all means, but do not try and shoehorn an unsuitable timbre into your arrangement. Number 6 is obviously problematic in that you will not have any recorded live vocal performances in your arrangement (it must all be sequenced), but it may be used to create a rhythm (from the speech rhythm) for either a new melody or a rhythm part. It would also be possible to use a sample of a **short** lyrical fragment that you could then manipulate in your arrangement. It would not be a good idea to base your whole arrangement around this – it would be better used as a minor production element. Always check that the use of samples is permitted in the year of your examination (by checking on the front of the stimulus material booklet provided by Edexcel) before using them in your arrangement.

1) Melodic signposts

Analyse the melody of the stimulus song and circle any short motifs that are instantly recognisable. This may be as short as three notes or as long as a whole phrase, but the shorter the better. Go through the whole stimulus locating any of these melodic motifs you feel are memorable – there are likely to be one or two in the verse and another one or two in the chorus (the middle 8 may not contain any instantly recognisable motifs). List them in whatever form of notation you find easiest.

Remember to include the audio track in your research here – the notated stimulus may not include some of the recognisable instrumental melodies.

Riffs are also melodic signposts – they are generally strong melodies played on an instrument. Treat these in the same way as sung melodies.

2) Harmonic signposts

Are there any particular chord sequences, chord changes or even individual chords that stand out in the given stimulus? Not all songs have a strong enough or individual enough chord sequence for this to be applicable, so you may discover that you would need the whole chord sequence to recognise the stimulus song. This is fine – write it down.

3) Rhythmic signposts

The most instantly recognisable rhythms will be in the drum part, but do not neglect the rhythms in the melodic parts or accompaniment parts that may also be rather memorable.

If you struggle to write out the rhythms, try playing them into a sequencing package or simply refer to the point in the song where the rhythm occurs.

Research covers and remixes

Find as many cover versions and remixes of the stimulus song as you can. Music download sites are a great resource for this as you can search for a particular song title and will immediately be presented with all the available options. You do not necessarily have to buy the tracks – the 29-second preview time might be enough to give you an idea of how the artist has treated the original material.

Has the cover version used the same ideas you spotted when looking for the signposts? If so, how has the new artist dealt with them? Has it simply been restated with a different backing or has it been developed in some way? List any interesting development techniques you unearth in your search. Has the new artist found other aspects of the stimulus song interesting? If so, list these under the appropriate signposts.

Place the signposts in a new context

Some of the 'signposts' will work well within the new context of your chosen style, and some will either need a significant amount of tweaking or will not work at all in the new context. Go through the signposts you have listed and try them out in the new style to decide which ones work straight away and which ones will need some tinkering.

The tightrope

You are walking a tightrope between developing the ideas from the original material enough in order to score the highest available marks in the optional criteria and making sure that there is enough of the signpost left intact to point the way to the original stimulus song. Remember – this is an arranging task, not a composing task, so the idea is to ensure it is obvious what the original stimulus was while still coming up with a new and interesting piece of music. However, neither is it a remixing task where you take the existing melodic idea, chop it into fragments and put a new beat and accompaniment parts to it – you have to walk the tightrope between these extremes in order to be successful.

You have spent some time listing all the different features of your chosen style, so should know what the important 'fingerprints' of the style are. Develop the 'signposts' you have listed from the stimulus song so that they fit comfortably within the constraints of the new style. Remember that you do not need to cover all criteria in the mark scheme – this is why you considered question 9 of the logbook at the beginning of this task – you only need to ensure you are able to score the top marks in three of the optional criteria, so concentrate on the three areas that are most appropriate to the chosen style and are most possible with the signposts you have selected from the stimulus material.

If you are still unsure of ways in which you might develop the musical material, turn to the section on developing musical ideas for unit 3C (page 128) to get some hints.

Completing the logbook

You will have spent a great deal of time researching the chosen style and considering ways in which to develop the stimulus material, so a lot of the work for this section is already complete.

Questions 7 and 8

These are very similar to questions 1 and 2 referring to task 1A. Complete questions 7 and 8 in the same way, listing the equipment and software used, listing any samples used (and what you have done to develop them) and giving any additional details you feel are appropriate to draw the examiner's attention to specific points.

Questions 9 and 10

These are worth 10 marks each (20 marks in total). Your arrangement is worth 40 marks. Although you will not spend half the time completing these two questions as you did completing the actual arrangement, it is well worth remembering that these two questions carry half the marks that are available for each of the practical tasks. Take your time and ensure that you claim the marks that are waiting for you here. There are no marks available for any of the rest of the logbook, but it will help to draw the examiner's attention to various aspects of the practical tasks, thus gaining you credit elsewhere.

Both questions have references in the mark schemes to the quality of written communication (QWC). This means that your answers to the questions must be coherent, showing that you have planned out the answer itself – note that this does not refer to planning out task 1C – it is showing that you have planned the response to questions 9 and 10. You must also present your answers with as few spelling mistakes as possible, using grammatically correct language. It is possible to answer in bullet points or note form, so you should not feel that you have to answer the questions in continuous prose if this is something that would cause you concern.

Question 9 asks how you have developed your arrangement from the stimulus song. You should refer not just to the requested two features, but the three features you think would be most appropriate as the optional criteria when the examiner assesses your work. Remember that the examiner who reads this logbook will also be marking your arrangement, so this is another opportunity to show why you ought to be given marks in your arrangement! Your answer should include details of how you have developed the signpost material as well as how you placed it into the context of the chosen style.

Question 10 should now be an easy one – you have identified many aspects of the chosen style already – all you have to do is narrow it down to those aspects you think are most important, making sure that these are the ones you have actually used in your arrangement. There is no point talking about features of the chosen style that you have decided to leave out of your arrangement, not least because it will just draw the examiner's attention to the fact that they are missing!

What can I expect in the exam?

There will be six questions in the exam, split into two sections for a total of 80 marks. Section A will contain four questions and will carry 40 marks (each question is worth 10 marks). Section B will contain two questions and will also carry 40 marks (each question is worth 20 marks). Area of study 1: the principles and practice of music technology and area of study 2: popular music styles since 1910 will be examined in this unit. Overall, unit 2 is worth 30% of the AS or 15% of the full GCE. The examination will be taken in May/June of the AS year and it will last for 1 hour and 45 minutes.

The following table summarises the contents of the examination paper for unit 2:

	Section A	Section B	Unit 2 Summary
Question Number	1–4	5–6	6 questions
Area of Study	1 and 2	1 and 2	AoS 1 and 2
Marks	40	40	80 Marks
% of AS	15%	15%	30% of AS

All the questions refer to music on an audio CD to be provided by Edexcel for the examination. You will need access to an individual CD player and headphones.

What will the questions ask?

You will be asked questions on the various aspects of the music and the technology used in the music. There will be a variety of question types including some or all of the following:

- Multiple choice
- Single-word response
- Short response
- Extended response
- Fill in the blanks
- Complete the table
- Staff notation
- Complete the rhythm
- Select the correct rhythm
- Complete the melody
- Select the correct melody
- Complete/annotate the arrange page/edit window.

Section A: Questions 1–4

Section A will test your ability to hear different musical characteristics or the use of music technology in the recordings on the audio CD provided. All the questions will be on music taken from area of study 2: popular music styles since 1910.

All the questions will be split into several parts, looking at different aspects of the music. There will be questions on the general musical characteristics (elements of music) in the song and questions on the production and arrangement from a music technology point of view.

Questions on the musical elements will include the following:

- Timbre: Naming the instruments used or describing the sound of an unfamiliar instrument
- Texture: Describing the way the parts are combined in the songs
- Pitch: Filling in the missing notes in staff notation or selecting the correct melody in a multiple choice context
- Tonality: Recognising the difference between major and minor
- Rhythm: Filling in missing rhythms in staff notation or selecting the correct rhythm in a multiple choice context, or dealing with specific rhythm parts common to a certain style
- Time signatures: Recognising and understanding these both aurally and on staff notation
- Tempo: Metronome markings and tempo changes (gradual or sudden)
- General understanding of instrumental playing techniques (such as electric guitar techniques/drum techniques)
- General understanding of these elements as they relate to different musical styles.

Questions on production and arrangement will include the following:

- Effects: Naming prominent effects used on different parts and describing various parameters of these effects
- Processors: Describing the use of processing in a given track or discussing where it might be used to improve the audio
- Production techniques: Analysing specific production techniques used in the audio tracks
- Arrangement techniques: Analysing the arrangement of the song and discussing how/why it was put together the way it is
- Recording techniques: General questions on how you might record an instrument in a given context
- Sequencing packages: Questions on the appropriate use of different editors
- MIDI: A knowledge of how MIDI works and its possible uses in the audio tracks
- General understanding of the use of music technology as it relates to different musical styles.

The questions in this section will draw on the knowledge you have gained on the practical use of music technology during your experiences of tackling the practical work for music portfolio 1. They will also draw from area of study 2: popular music styles since 1910, but in a general way rather than requiring detailed knowledge of every pop music style in the 20th and 21st centuries.

Section B: Questions 5–6

Questions in section B will cover similar ground to those in section A with one fundamental difference – section B will ask questions related to the special focus styles. The questioning styles will be similar, but there will always be a section at the end of each question requiring more extended writing (10–12 lines) on some area of the special focus style. There is no choice of questions in section B – you must complete both questions, each of which is worth 20 marks. Question 5 will look at one of the special focus styles and question 6 will look at the other.

There is likely to be a question on some aspect of the context of one of the special focus styles – this could be to do with the social and cultural conditions surrounding the development of the style or questions on the main influences of the style, for example. There will be questions on specific, popular artists who have been associated with the special focus style.

What do I need to know?

- ○ Area of study 1: the principles and practice of music technology
- ○ Area of study 2: popular music styles since 1910.

Area of study 1: the principles and practice of music technology

While you were completing your practical work for unit 1, you were learning how to use a sequencing package, edit sounds, use different types of microphone, operate a mixing desk, apply effects to a sound, mix tracks down to stereo and many other things. This knowledge forms the basis of area of study 1. You should also learn other techniques that were used in certain musical styles, whether you used them yourself or not. This is especially true of the special focus styles – there may be specific production techniques that were used in a certain style that help to identify it as that style (for example, the use of a particular effect, or a specific microphone technique used to capture the instruments).

Area of study 2: popular music styles since 1910

This area of study requires you to study popular music from the year 1910 to the present. However, there is nothing particularly special about the year 1910, so for the purposes of this book, we shall split popular music into two main sections – pre-rock and roll and post-rock and roll.

The main problem with the study of any musical style is that there is a significant crossover between all styles, more grey areas than black and white, and many styles that seem to be fairly distinct include a significant element of cross-fertilisation of ideas and influences. Instead of fighting against this immutable fact, we need to embrace it and study music, especially popular music, as a whole with different, interweaving strands. Imagine a tub of white paint into which you pour a little blue, red and yellow paint at different points in the tub. If you stir it a little, there will be places that are still white, some that are distinctly blue, red or yellow, but most of the paint will have turned some shade of pink, orange, green or purple. The same is true of music – we have a certain amount of basic musical ingredients to play with, and some very original artists take things to a different level, but most artists are somewhere in between.

So why study musical styles at all?

Most artists do not like to be put into a box. They want to be originals producing music that has not been heard before and not thought of as lumped in with other bands and singers they don't particularly like. However, the very fact that they use the same instrumental line-up as other bands, playing the same sort of guitar riffs at a similar volume in the same time signature begs comparison with the similar bands. Isn't it nice to be able to walk to the correct section of a music store to get directly to the music you want? You do not necessarily want to sift through the Motörhead back catalogue before you get to the Mozart symphonies!

In order to place a piece of music within a certain style, it needs to be broken down to its component parts – you need to analyse the rhythm, groove, melody, harmony, instrumentation, production, tonality, lyrics, texture etc. to see if these aspects are similar to those used by other bands and artists. The process of this analysis forces you to listen to a song on a deeper level. If you develop your ear to the extent that you are listening for a specific reverb type on a snare drum, or a particular type of synth sound, it means you can appreciate music on a new level, even if you do not enjoy the song itself. The process of breaking music down to its component parts also assists the composition process – if you can hear how other people put their music together you can start by emulating them, recognising their use of the musical ingredients and then add something new to make your piece original.

Popular music

Popular music, by definition, is the music that is popular at any given point in time. This means that pop music in general is fashionable, faddy and disposable. Through the decades, there have been times when the popular music of the day has had some serious content in one form or another, either lyrically or musically, but in general, pop music tends to steer a middle-of-the-road, inoffensive (or deliberately offensive), saccharine path to mass product sales. This means that the popular music of any given era tends to be a safe amalgam of the musical tastes of the time and often avoids being placed squarely into one style or another – the songs are just pop songs that make it into the charts. If you go through a list of number one hits over the last three decades, you are likely to recognise or remember less than one in twenty of them. The ones that you do remember are those that really stuck out – the Bohemian Rhapsodies of this world. In fact, sometimes the really great songs were kept off the number one spot by some piece of forgettable, anonymous, manufactured pop that spun out of the hit factory of a production team set up to deliver chart success. This is the way of pop music and the entertainment industry in general!

However, when defining styles, we are looking at artists who, instead of releasing an album to back up a hit single and then vanishing into obscurity, deliberately carved a niche for themselves in such a way that they attracted a loyal fan base. These are the pioneers that make pop music possible – they sail uncharted waters and tame previously untamed musical elements making it possible for something to become middle-of-the-road a decade down the line that would have been cutting edge and daring originally.

Pre-rock and roll

There has always been music that is more popular than other music since the concept of music was invented, but for the purposes of the GCE Music Technology specification, we are starting near the beginning of the 20th century. At this time, something very important is going on in the south of the US – the birth of jazz.

- ○ Birth of jazz
- ○ Ragtime
- ○ Early blues
- ○ Tin Pan Alley
- ○ Jazz moves north
- ○ Swing
- ○ Modern jazz styles
- ○ Rock and roll.

Birth of jazz

During the 1800s, New Orleans was a thriving town containing a real mix of cultures. Between its founding and the early 1800s it had changed hands between the French, Spanish and the US, and so had its share of French and Spanish settlers. At the beginning of the 1800s, many people moved north to New Orleans from the Caribbean to flee oppressive regimes. There were many settlers from other European nations such as England, Ireland and Germany who moved to New Orleans for business or to start a new life in the New World. The town was a hub of commerce, with riverboats running along the main artery of the Mississippi river, providing trade and business opportunities galore. Many traders from all parts of the world travelled through New Orleans, with some deciding to settle there. There was also a significant population of black slaves brought to America from West Africa, some coming via the Caribbean. At the end of the 19th century, the railroad began to take over from the riverboats as the main method of travel and transport, so New Orleans began to fall into decline. As New Orleans' fortunes diminished, the cultural mix was gradually stirred in the basin of the Mississippi delta.

All the cultures brought with them some aspects of their own music and, in living together, they made music together, thus bringing together elements of Caribbean, African and European music and mixing it with a healthy dose of Creole, brass band, ragtime, gospel, early blues and country music along with many other, less distinct influences. While some of these influences survived intact, others gelled together to form a completely new style that was to become known as New Orleans Jazz.

New Orleans Jazz ensembles featured some front line (lead) instruments, all improvising melodies at the same time over a chord sequence to form an improvised counterpoint. Commonly these instruments would include the cornet and trombone from the New Orleans brass band tradition and the clarinet. They would generally be accompanied by a chordal instrument such as the banjo or piano and may or may not include drums (the banjo also acted as a time-keeper, chugging away on the beat).

Ragtime

Meanwhile, in the late 19th and early 20th centuries, the piano was becoming increasingly popular in the US as a chamber instrument. In the days before mass media it was impossible to hear music unless you went to a venue where someone was performing or produced the music yourself, so the piano was a great option – it allows the production of melodies and an accompaniment in one instrument. As such, the market was ripe for anyone who produced sheet music that could be performed on the piano. Ragtime music rather snugly filled this gap in the market.

Ragtime is an intoxicating mix of on-the-beat, left hand broken chords in an 'oompah' style, alternating between the root or 5th low down in the bass register and a block chord in the middle register, and a syncopated melody, sometimes played in octaves, higher up in the piano's range. The music was full of life and rhythmic energy, and the nature of the accompaniment part in the left hand made it sound very full and musically satisfying as well as presenting a challenge to budding pianists all over the country. Successful ragtime composers could sell hundreds of thousands of copies of their sheet music to the general public. The most famous of the ragtime composers was Scott Joplin (1868–1917), who wrote *Maple Leaf Rag* and *The Entertainer* among many other well-known rags. Player-pianos were also popular at this time, where piano rolls activated a mechanism for the hammers to hit the strings, thus allowing the piano to play itself without the need for a physical performer. Ragtime was very popular for this medium.

Perhaps more than anything else, the popularity of ragtime across the whole of the US made it possible for jazz music to be widely accepted.

Early blues

Blues developed in the deep south of the US at the end of the 19th century as music of protest, despair and hope. It originated as music of the African-American slaves.

Blues grew out of the slaves' work songs – songs sung while working, partly as a way to keep a rhythm going in repetitive manual activity such as digging, partly as a way of making the hours go by. The songs were call and response style with someone leading the rest of the work gang. After the emancipation of the black slaves at the end of the American civil war, work songs continued with railroad work gangs and chain gangs from jails, doing their manual labour. The melodies for these songs contain an interesting phenomenon called 'blue-notes'. These notes arose as a way of reconciling the pentatonic melodies of Africa with the seven-note melodies of western hymn tunes that had been taught to the slaves as a way of converting and controlling them. The use of hymn tunes is also important, because many of the religious lyrics made their way into early gospel and blues. The songs, sometimes relating to the Israelites' journey under Moses' leadership from Egypt to the Promised Land, were looking forward to better times (music of hope) while protesting about present conditions and crying out in despair about a poverty-stricken existence. The sense of being down or feeling melancholic was known as being 'blue', hence the name given to the musical style. Singing the blues helped in a cathartic way to get emotions out and make life seem a little better.

Ex-slaves were able to use instruments to add accompaniment to their songs (they were previously forbidden, or at least discouraged, from any form of music making other than work songs by plantation bosses and the like), but they were still very poor, so tended to use whatever was to hand – old, half-broken guitars with only a few strings left, tapping feet on the ground to provide a bass drum beat, and anything else they could lay their hands on. Music making has always been at the core of African society, so the music making of the ex-slaves started to make a comeback. Some musicians used old bottlenecks to play the guitars, neutralising the problem of a lack of strings (notice how making the best of what you have can force creative solutions – one to remember for your arranging or composing work). The bottleneck style also helped them to imitate vocal-like sounds, slides and scoops – an important aspect of blues to this day.

Blues was often built around a three-line lyric where the first line was repeated and a third line answered the first two lines. The 12-bar blues structure originated from giving each of these lines four bars (singing and then responding with the instrument playing a fill at the end of the phrase) but, in practise, since many of the musicians would be accompanying themselves singing, the blues was anything but 12-bars – it could be anywhere from 9 to 16 bars, with any number in between depending on how they felt at the time! The melodies were generally pentatonic with additional blue notes adding a 'wailing' element, and played over very simple harmonies based around a tonic chord with the possible addition of a second or third chord. The harmonies eventually developed into the 'three chord trick' we are now familiar with. Blues was a major contributor to the origins of jazz music, but it also continued its development alongside jazz (and ragtime). It remained music performed mostly by African-Americans, whereas jazz had quite a few white performers, almost from its very beginnings.

Tin Pan Alley

At the turn of the century, popular music making consisted mostly of vaudeville and light opera (operetta). Vaudeville had the more risqué songs, and operetta (such as Gilbert and Sullivan) was the domain of the middle-classes. At the start of the 1900s, due to the popularity of the piano in American homes, there was a massive demand for sheet music, so composers would write songs for the purpose of distribution by this medium. The songs could come from the vaudeville or operetta tradition, but increasingly they were being written by composers solely for the purpose of sheet music sales. The industry, centred mostly on Broadway in New York (and, to a lesser extent, the west end), came to be known as 'Tin Pan Alley', with piano music adorned with sentimental, sugary lyrics distributed for the masses. From the first world war to the end of the second world war there was also a demand for patriotic songs, which was fulfilled by Tin Pan Alley (with songs such as 'It's a Long Way to Tipperary' and 'The White Cliffs of Dover').

Jazz moves north

New Orleans jazz did not become truly popular until musicians such as Jelly Roll Morton, King Oliver and Louis Armstrong moved north to Chicago and New York just after WWI. Louis Armstrong led the way in the transition from New Orleans to Chicago jazz – the soloist (often the band-leader) took centre stage and the other musicians were clearly supporting him as opposed to the equal roles the front line play in New Orleans jazz.

Ragtime had already paved the way for the acceptance of black music from the deep south, so jazz quickly became part of the popular music scene of the 1920s.

Alongside the development of Chicago jazz and the virtuoso soloist idea through the 1920s was the growth of bands from the five or six pieces common in New Orleans ensembles. As the bands grew it became less practical for everyone to solo or to improvise even simple lines at the same time, so the need for arranging the parts became apparent. This opened the way for the great jazz arrangers and band-leaders such as Duke Ellington who would produce notated parts for the performers to play. The bands they led became known simply as 'big bands', playing 'big band jazz'. Although there was much more emphasis on the arrangement and interplay of the different sections (reeds, brass and percussion), the top soloists were still very much in demand to play as part of the bands, so they could take the solo slots in the arrangements (8 or 16 bar solo breaks were essential parts of the arrangements for the top performers to strut their stuff). Some performers made a name for themselves because of their tasteful or skilful soloing in a big band setup (such as Bix Beiderbecke and Benny Carter), many of who went on to front their own band. Big band jazz developed as a popular form of entertainment in nightclubs for dances with resident bands in New York nightclubs featuring guest soloists and vocalists. The band needed to be a certain size to fill the venue, hence the need to boost the numbers of players. To maintain the popular status, it was important that the arrangers included arrangements of Tin Pan Alley songs, or songs influenced by Tin Pan Alley, so the use of 32-bar song forms became more common than the use of 12-bar blues and ragtime structures.

Swing

The Great Depression of the early 1930s hit everyone hard, including musicians, but by 1935, the medium of radio offered people an escape from day-to-day life. Radio was the perfect medium for big band jazz music, with Benny Goodman (band leader and clarinettist) appearing regularly on a program called 'Let's Dance'. Goodman was white, and was perhaps more readily accepted by the white audience, leading to an explosion in the popularity of jazz. Bandleaders like Goodman, Ellington and Fletcher Henderson developed their big bands into radio-friendly outfits, playing songs that would be immediately popular with the masses. This offered great opportunities for the arrangers to showcase their skills, the best arrangers being in great demand. The big band music of the late 1930s became known as 'swing', and was the popular music of the day. People who went out to dances expected to dance to a swing band performing the latest swing hits of the day. 1935–1945 are widely recognised as the golden years of jazz, when jazz music was at its most popular. Of course, this meant that some rather sanitised arrangements were produced for the swing bands, with little opportunity for the talented improvisers to display their talent, so those who wanted to move in this direction were forced to find another outlet.

Modern jazz styles

The Glenn Miller big band marked the beginning of the end for the swing era – there was no longer any room for soloing and his hits tended to have much more in common with the Tin Pan Alley numbers than they did with the jazz of New Orleans and Chicago. Talented improvisers such as Charlie Parker (alto sax), Dizzy Gillespie (trumpet), Charlie Christian (guitar) and Thelonius Monk (piano) started meeting in various clubs around Harlem, jamming well into the small hours of the morning. Their music was hard hitting, in-your-face improvisation, played at high speed over advanced chord sequences. The music they created became known as 'bebop'. People who came to hear the bebop musicians came to listen to good musicianship, not to dance, so it did not have the same mass appeal or money-spinning potential as swing music. This was the beginning of modern jazz, marking a divergence in jazz styles where different creative individuals would take the music in different directions. New jazz styles included 'cool' jazz, 'modal' jazz, and fusion.

Rock 'n' roll

So, what happened to blues? Well, it was about to burst on to the scene in a big way, but up until the early 1950s, blues was music played by black people for black people to listen to in very localised scenes. Similarly, country music was played by white people, generally in the southern states, for white people to listen to. Both styles had radio stations dedicated to them, but these were set up to serve the communities in which the music flourished. The major population centres had not really accepted blues or country yet, preferring to listen to swing, or swing derived music, and Tin Pan Alley-style sentimental songs. This appealed to those who were still suffering the austere atmosphere of the post-war years and who had memories of the great depression – it still served as escapism, but for the young people of the post-war generation, it left something of a gap.

Blues had by now developed into R&B (rhythm and blues) – blues played on electric instruments (electric guitar and bass) with a clearly defined structure (often borrowing from the swing jazz style) and a more driving beat, designed for dancing to and therefore for a wider audience than early blues. It had also spread north to Chicago, where it became known as Chicago blues and took on a much harder edge than the rural, southern blues. Artists such as Muddy Waters and Howlin' Wolf were using electric instruments, with a drum kit supplying the rhythmic drive. Guitar players such as B. B. King and Buddy Guy introduced the guitar as a lead instrument in blues, much like Charlie Christian had done in jazz – since the guitar could now be amplified, the tone sustained for longer and could thus be made to 'sing' like the front line horns in jazz combos. However, this music was still very much African-American music and a little too hard-edged and raw for the majority of the white audience.

An early fusion of the white country music of the rural south and black blues is 'rockabilly', championed by Carl Perkins. He described the music as 'blues with a country beat' – it emphasised beats two and four, used the electric guitar and an upright bass (double bass), played very aggressively so that the strings would slap rhythmically against the fingerboard producing a percussive sound. Elvis' first recordings for Sun Records in 1954 were in this style, but it was not long before he was snapped up by RCA (in 1956) and became involved in the rock 'n' roll revolution.

In 1954, Bill Haley and the Comets released the song 'Rock Around the Clock'. It became a worldwide phenomenon, selling more than 15 million copies. This was the song that marked the start of rock 'n' roll as the new popular music. Rock 'n' roll had been developing for a few years before this (to a certain extent evolving from rockabilly), when rhythm and blues started to be played on predominately white radio stations, but Bill Haley's track is credited for starting the rock 'n' roll craze in the youth of America.

Rock 'n' roll stood for rebellion, it offered young people a music that was much more rhythmically exciting than anything Tin Pan Alley had to offer, had lyrics that often made reference to sexual themes, used loud electric instruments, threw up a number of key performers with great charisma who went against what was thought of as being 'decent' (for example, Elvis and his famous hip gyrations) and, above all, it met with the universal disapproval of the older generation. All these ingredients spelt instant commercial success and sparked off a revolution amongst young people of the time. It was a chance to throw off the austerity of the post-war years and for the younger generation to find its own identity.

Some artists closely associated with rock 'n' roll include:

- Bill Haley (and the Comets)
- Buddy Holly
- Chuck Berry
- Elvis Presley
- Jerry Lee Lewis
- Little Richard.

Rock 'n' roll recordings make extensive use of 'slap-back' echo, particularly on the vocal and electric guitar parts. Slap-back echo is a very short delay (approx 80ms) with one repeat, but with much of the high frequency rolled off (this was a consequence of the technology of the time in that delay units used tape devices with terrible specs, but is emulated nowadays by filtering out the high frequencies). Original rock 'n' roll recordings are generally found on mono vinyl records – stereo recordings were not issued commercially until 1958.

Rock and roll has been used to describe many kinds of music, from 1950s rock 'n' roll to the hard rock of bands like AC/DC, but when the GCE Music Technology specification refers to rock and roll, it is referring to the rock 'n' roll music popular from 1954–59.

Post rock 'n' roll

Now that black music had been introduced into the mainstream through rock 'n' roll, there was nothing to hold it back. Teenagers had found a culture and were now a commercial resource to be tapped by record companies.

- Britain in the 1960s
- Soul
- Funk
- Reggae
- Rap and hip-hop
- Rock in the late 1960s
- Heavy rock
- Punk and new wave
- Indie rock
- Club dance.

Britain in the 1960s

But what of Britain? All the popular music discussed so far (with the sidelined exception of West End-penned Tin Pan Alley hits and patriotic songs) has been very much an American phenomenon. Britain found its voice in the 1960s.

In the 1950s a style known as 'skiffle' emerged – a jazz-influenced sound using readily available objects such as a washboard as a rhythm section and a home-made bass made from a broom handle and string along with a guitar or a banjo. This was not overly important in itself, but John Lennon's Quarrymen were a skiffle band, influencing the sound of the Beatles. Skiffle bands were influenced by the sounds of rock 'n' roll and R&B, with musicians turning to electric instruments. By the start of the 1960s these styles merged in bands such as the Beatles and Gerry and the Pacemakers to form 'British Beat' (sometimes interchangeable with the term 'Merseybeat' because much of the music was centred on Liverpool).

At the end of the 1950s, as the rock 'n' roll era drew to a close, British music lovers began to turn to black R&B from the US. The scarcity, or prohibitive price of imported records available pushed some musicians into making their own music, imitating the sound of American R&B. Initially these attempts were doomed to failure, but soon some very able musicians took the American sound and gave it a British flavour, so that the style they came up with became known as 'British R&B'. Bands such as the Rolling Stones, the Yardbirds and John Mayall's Bluesbreakers were examples of British R&B. These bands started the 'British invasion' – British bands became very popular, not just in Britain, but also in America. So much so that American bands began to imitate the British imitation of American R&B!

'Mod' culture burst onto the scene in Britain around 1963. Short for 'modernist', it reflected British youth's rejection of what they saw as the bland, old-fashioned culture in which they existed. They wanted to embrace anything they saw as being 'hip', which meant American R&B and soul, as well as Jamaican ska. Mod culture had a strict dress code, depending on the situation (parkas for riding the ubiquitous scooters and smart suits for night life). The Who and the Small Faces were seen as groups that reflected the mod ideology.

Soul

Although black R&B began to get some airtime on white radio stations in the early 1950s, it was largely still a localised music, played on black radio stations and released through local, independent record labels (i.e. record labels who were not part of the major labels such as RCA, Columbia and Decca). In 1960, in Memphis, the label Stax was set up (later gaining a distribution deal with Atlantic records to get Stax artists nationwide coverage) using an in-house band as backing for several different vocalists. This in-house band became Booker T. and the MGs. Stax recordings were aimed primarily at the black R&B audience, sporting gospel influenced vocals and clean, tight arrangements. Some artists who recorded for the Stax label include:

- Booker T. and the MGs
- Otis Redding
- Sam and Dave.

At the same time, in Detroit (called motor town because of the automotive industry present in the city), another label was set up called Motown. Motown was aimed more at a white audience, so its recordings tended to be much more commercial than Stax music so as to fit into the charts.

Some artists who recorded for Motown include:

- The Four Tops
- The Supremes
- The Temptations.

Music from the two labels became known as Stax and Motown music, but both of them were developments of R&B that would later fall under the umbrella label of 'soul'. Marvin Gaye and Stevie Wonder both grew out of the Motown stable, bringing soul music into the 1970s.

Other soul artists include:

- Otis Redding
- Aretha Franklin
- Wilson Pickett
- Percy Sledge
- James Brown (also associated with funk).

The music was written to have a soulful sound, but to be easy to dance to (making it a forerunner for disco). It had a tight rhythm section, often complimented by a horn section (trumpets, sax and sometimes trombone), playing tight, arranged, rhythmic stabs to punctuate the music. Often the brass section would play the main riff along with, or instead of the guitar which was sometimes relegated more to a time-keeping instrument, playing on the off-beats. The rhythms were influenced by the newly developing funk sound (championed by James Brown), but the gospel-style vocals can clearly be heard in Aretha Franklin's work, amongst others. Some styles of soul, especially towards the end of the 1960s and the start of the 1970s (such as Philly, or Philadelphia soul), would have lush string arrangements over which the singers could deliver their lines. Soul music was often about love, and tended to have rather emotional lyrics, but as the 1960s progressed several singers became more politically active, supporting the civil rights movements. Motown tried to distance itself from the political scene because its commercial interests were dependent on sales in the white community.

Funk

James Brown was a notoriously hard band leader, working his musicians very hard to get the exact sound he wanted. Anyone who graduated from Brown's backing bands was going to be able to hold down a tight rhythm. In 1972 Bootsy and Catfish Collins (Bass and rhythm guitar respectively) joined George Clinton's outfit Parliament/Funkadelic after they had quit James Brown's backing band (he had two bands, partly for legal reasons, and partly because they boasted two different styles, even though they had mostly the same members). They formed a formidable rhythm section when teamed up with a good drummer, locking into 'grooves' that were much more important than the melodies or chord sequences. In fact, many of the chords in the guitar part would be high voicings of 9ths and other extended or altered chords, but they gave the sound a distinctive 'chop'. The sound of George Clinton's ensemble was the definitive sound of funk in the early 1970s, influencing many other styles from jazz to metal. Other important funk outfits include Kool and the Gang and Earth, Wind and Fire.

Reggae

While the rock 'n' roll revolution was happening in the US, the British colonial government was preparing to leave Jamaica (the island gained its independence in 1962). In Jamaica, music was enjoyed either by listening to live bands or to sound systems. Sound systems were a culture onto themselves – they were both mobile PA rigs, but also the main form of recording industry on the island – records were cut specifically for the sound systems, with great competition between soundmen to have the next new thing. The soundmen/DJs ran their own dances with their sound systems, keeping a close contact with their audience, and giving the music a sense of immediacy. Such a close relationship with the audience meant that there was a will to promote home-grown music. By keeping the disks they had cut for their own sound system for their own audience for a few months before they would let it be released to the general public, DJs built up a sense of loyalty and a certain hype for when the song was eventually released!

To begin with, in the 1950s, the music that was popular on the island was the American R&B that some were able to pick up on their radios from American radio stations, but there was a hunger for something new. There were good musicians on the island who went to the US to learn and ply their trade. By the start of the 1960s, the musicians were beginning to find that there was work to be found at home now that R&B was becoming so popular. R&B quickly fused with the rhythms of mento – a Jamaican folk music style similar to calypso – and the big band jazz style line up to form a new style, indigenous to Jamaica called 'ska'. Ska was very popular in the nightclubs, with lots of horn players in the bands (many from the big band jazz tradition), revelling in the freedom of playing their own music instead of being constrained to the, by now, tired formula of the big band sound – they still had the 'cutting contests' of jazz, where they would try to out-solo each other, but it was all based on a strong rhythmic foundation from the fusion of mento and R&B. There wasn't a lot of room for vocals in ska, although songs did feature vocalists from time to time, but it was mainly an energetic, instrumental music. The mood of independence and freedom on the island at the time worked its way into the joyful sound of ska. The Skatalites were one of the first bands to be a successful recorded export of the ska sound.

By the mid 1960s, the influence of American soul music was felt in Jamaica. The vocal-oriented music soon fused with ska to form a more commercial sound called 'rock steady'. Rock steady was especially influenced by the soul bands featuring close harmony work (such as The Impressions), so three-part vocal harmony is one of the features of the new, radio-friendly style.

DJs would always boast about how good their sound system was, calling it the biggest and best, that they were playing the best music and so on. During the 1960s, this boasting took on a rhythmic function, with DJs 'bigging up' their sound systems at the start of the record, speaking in time to the music. Talking over the music developed into a form called 'toasting' where the DJ would interact with the lyrics on the record, or toast rhythmically over the song to hype up the audience.

The act of recycling music was a trait much loved by DJs. They would take a song and fade the vocal in and out (or remove it altogether), playing the studio like an instrument, adding echo, reverbs and any other effect they could find to the instrumental mix and snippets of the original vocal lines. If they reduced the amount of vocal on the record, it gave them much more space to toast over without having to compete with the original vocal line. This remixing culture grew into a musical style in its own right called 'Dub'. The widely acknowledged king of dub was King Tubby, a genius with electronics, who would customise his studio equipment so he could achieve completely original effects. His skills were always in great demand.

By the end of the 1960s, rock steady had taken on many of the American soul and R&B traits, with some Jamaicans concerned that it had lost its identity. The time was ripe for change, so the sound systems connected with the public again playing bass-heavy, more up-tempo music featuring rhythmic stabs from the electric organ and choppy guitar chords, reminiscent of the banjo in mento. The electric bass had been used before but it was now made into a feature of the new music that was to become known as reggae.

Rude-boy culture sprang up in the late 1960s, with gang culture beginning to dominate the music scene. There had always been some violence at dances, but the rude-boys upped the ante by bringing weapons and running protection rackets. Then, by 1972, people were beginning to feel the pinch of some government decisions and the British withdrawal from the country, so there was a growing unrest. Rastafarianism had been present in Jamaica for a long time, but the social climate of the early 1970s made it grow all the quicker. Into this scene came artists such as Bob Marley, The Mighty Diamonds and Burning Spear. They introduced a new reggae style known as 'roots reggae', preaching the evils of Babylon (white dominance) and bringing a heightened political awareness to their song lyrics. Marley was to become reggae's main export to the rest of the world, with many of his songs covered by artists in different styles. His untimely death in 1981 was heralded as the end of reggae, but actually it just served to boost his reputation to that of a legend, with Marley selling considerably more albums after his death than in his lifetime.

Rap and hip-hop

Toasting has been around in black society for a long time, becoming important in the evolution of Reggae, so it wasn't something new, but there were not many examples of recorded toasting available – it tended to be a live, spontaneous thing. So, when Jalad Nuriddin of the Last Poets recorded 'Hustler's Convention' in 1973 in which he toasted over a funky rhythmic backing provided by Kool and the Gang, it was an important event. The toasting was tame by today's standards, but it was new for the time. Also in 1973, a Jamaican DJ called Kool Herc threw his first 'party in the park', bringing the reggae-style toasting to New York, and the black DJ, Afrika Bambaataa formed 'The Organisation', later to become 'Universal Zulu Nation'.

During the mid-1970s, a whole underground black culture was developing encompassing not only music, but also art and dance. By the late 1970s it was labelled 'hip-hop' and involved hip-hop music, graffiti art and breakdancing. The term 'rap' was coined later on by record companies (although the word itself was used in hip-hop lyrics previously). In the early years, the style developed in a similar way to reggae – the music was played at street parties by DJs, and very little made it onto record. The age-old problem of the record industry decision makers being predominately white meant that they were always reticent to take on any new black music. The other issue was that the record companies were aware that black youth did not have very much disposable income, so they were less likely to be able to make money from the music. The music was spread by the DJs recording tapes of their sets and distributing these by hand.

In 1975, the DJ Grand Wizard Theodore discovered a technique called 'scratching', where the record is spun by hand while the needle is still in contact with it, creating a scratching sound. This technique was to be developed by DJs to a very high skill level, such that the record deck became an instrument in its own right. The DJs would toast over the songs and would also mix elements of other music into the songs – the earliest examples of sampling. Eventually the record companies realised the potential of this new African-American music and decided to get in on the action. The Sugarhill gang became the first outfit to release a rap single with 'Rapper's Delight' in 1979.

Hip hop has always been keen to embrace technology, making extensive use of sampling, and to a certain extent, driving the development of sampling through the 1980s. Hip hop artists also made extensive use of drum machines. The 'old-school' style of rap was still based on toasting, so had a bit of a 'feel-good' factor to it, but by 1983 the lyrics started to depict the realities of life in the ghetto. By the mid-1980s, rap had crossed to white youth culture and was starting to be noticed internationally. In 1983, Run-DMC collaborated with the rock band Aerosmith on the single 'Walk this Way'. This resulted in the first real cross-over into the rock market (although this was to stall for some time before the 1990s when bands like Rage Against The Machine appeared).

As hip hop gradually became more mainstream, it started to break into various strands – some continuing in the mainstream and becoming slightly sanitised (for example MC Hammer) and others pushing the boundaries of acceptable behaviour in their use of swearing and lyrics about violence (gangsta rap). Hip hop has now become a catch-all label for a wide range of black music, including an increasing variety of styles.

Rock in the late 1960s

The end of the 1960s has been well documented as the time of hippies, flower-power, and the summer of love, so what was rock doing at the time?

- ○ Bob Dylan was busy enraging the folk community in 1965 by using electric guitars in his music, inventing 'urban folk' or 'folk rock'
- ○ Psychedelia was embraced by bands such as the Grateful Dead and Jefferson Airplane to create 'psychedelic rock'
- ○ Jimi Hendrix was taking the guitar world by storm, turning blues guitar into a rock phenomenon and experimenting with ways to increase the scope of the electric guitar
- ○ Progressive rock was taking its first, tentative steps into the world of combining the structures and harmonies of classical music and jazz with rock instrumentation and rhythms
- ○ Led Zeppelin and Deep Purple began riffing and soloing their way to creating heavy metal.

Heavy rock

In the 1960s, the concept of the guitar hero was born. Pete Townsend with his 'windmill' strum, smashing up his kit at the end of the show, Jimi Hendrix playing guitar with his teeth (and setting it on fire) and Eric Clapton being hailed as God by a graffiti artist – the guitarist had moved from the background to the front of the stage. Cream and The Who had been riffing through the 1960s, gradually getting more and more volume from their amplifiers – Townsend had been working alongside an engineer called Jim Marshall, who was designing bigger and louder amps for him with more distortion available. The guitar was getting louder and more prominent, allowing for louder, more aggressive riffing backed up by driving drums and bass.

There is little clear distinction between heavy rock and heavy metal. Although certain artists have tried to avoid certain labels, there is as much crossover in the world of loud, distorted, amplified guitar music as there is in any other musical style. Many of the bands would claim to be 'rock 'n' roll', but by saying this, they do not mean that they are the same genre as Chuck Berry, even if they are influenced by him, they are claiming to be part of a rock 'n' roll lifestyle. If there is any defining factor between metal and rock, it is in the harmonies used and the rhythms used in the accompaniment. Rock and heavy rock are very blues-orientated. For the majority of the time, riffs and solos are based on the pentatonic scale. The drum parts drive the ensemble, but they are not too complicated in themselves – a good rock drummer is able to hold a steady beat, but also lock into a groove, even while playing the simplest of rhythms. The bass guitar is a bridge between the riffing of the electric guitar and the steady thump of the bass drum – sometimes it will riff along with the guitar and sometimes it will pulse the root note, emphasising the rhythm of the bass drum. In essence, rock music in its purest form is supercharged, riff based blues.

Heavy metal tends to be more technically demanding in terms of instrumental ability, with much more use of minor scales and modes than rock. It will still make use of the pentatonic scale, but tends to add dissonances to the scale to give it a darker tone – such as emphasis on the flattened 5th as a dark-sounding interval, or use of the flattened 2nd. Both styles use 'power chords' – a chord consisting only of the root and the 5th of a chord, the absence of a major or minor 3rd making it possible to play riffs based on power chords as if they were single notes, giving a more powerful, thicker sound (hence the name, 'power chords'). Metal generally has much more demanding drum parts, with recent styles making extensive use of a double-bass pedal as a way to play much faster rhythms on the bass drum. Heavy metal-influenced styles also tend to detune the guitar, sometimes dropping the lowest string a tone – and sometimes tuning the whole guitar down a semitone or more – again to get a heavier, darker sound.

However, having listed these potential differences, different commentators use the terms interchangeably, so it is quite difficult to draw a clear distinction between the two styles.

Led Zeppelin, Deep Purple and Black Sabbath are commonly seen as the godfathers of heavy rock and heavy metal. However, on closer inspection, the bands have very distinctive sounds that influenced later bands in different ways. Led Zeppelin wrote many heavier songs, with some very famous and often-imitated riffs, but a large proportion of their output is actually quite folky – their guitarist, Jimmy Page was fond of using the acoustic guitar and mandolin on quite a few of their numbers. Deep Purple had a virtuoso keyboard player in Jon Lord, adding a different element to their instrumental texture – he was classically trained and was just as likely to take big solos as was their guitarist Ritchie Blackmore. Blackmore was fond of using the harmonic minor scale in his soloing, meshing in better with Lord's harmonic repertoire than would have been the case with the standard pentatonic scale (hence they leant more towards metal than rock). Black Sabbath had an altogether darker sound than either Led Zeppelin or Deep Purple, with the guitarist Tony Iommi tuning his guitar down a semitone to accommodate his dark riffing. He was fond of dissonant intervals in his playing, to go along with the imagery the band liked to promote (as their name would suggest). The lead singer for Black Sabbath, Ozzy Osbourne, was famous for his on-stage antics including biting the head off a bat.

These three bands had an enormous impact on all metal and rock acts to follow them through the 1970s and on to the present day. Their sound was more powerful than anything that had been heard before, and they liked to play as loudly as they possibly could given the restrictions on the equipment they were using. Much of what followed for some time was more a refinement of what they had started than it was breaking new ground. Bands in the 1970s in the heavy rock mould included Queen, Van Halen, Aerosmith, and AC/DC. Rock bands became so popular that they could no longer play smaller venues because of the demand for concert tickets, so they started playing bigger and bigger venues until they started filling football stadiums.

In the 1980s there was a divergence in the styles of heavy rock/metal. In 1983, Metallica released their first album 'Kill 'em All' – to be hailed as the first thrash album. This took heavy metal in a much more aggressive direction, with very fast, low, chugging guitar riffs accompanied by high speed bass drum passages and technically difficult guitar solos. At the same time, the more commercial side of rock could be seen in bands like Bon Jovi, who became extremely popular with their 1986 album 'Slippery When Wet'. In Britain, the 'new wave of British heavy metal' ushered in bands such as Iron Maiden (with their twin lead guitars) who continued the Black Sabbath imagery focusing on the dark side of the fantasy world.

Other styles to spring from heavy rock and heavy metal include Death Metal (an extreme form of thrash), funk metal/rock (fusing funk rhythms with the riffing of rock) and progressive metal (the combination of the ideas of progressive rock with the energy and technical virtuosity of modern metal).

Punk and new wave

Progressive rock was one of the most popular styles of music in the early 1970s. It involved long, meandering structures, elongated solos and concept albums often based on fantasy worlds such as Tolkien's *Lord of the Rings*. At the same time, disco was becoming popular in Britain with its glitz and glitterballs. Considering the high unemployment rate and the economic problems in Britain at this time, it is not surprising that a sizeable proportion of the population felt that this music did not cater for where they were at. Out of this sense of discontentment sprang the aggressive, uncompromising sound of punk music.

In the early 1970s, The Velvet Underground, The Stooges and the New York Dolls were making music in the US that eschewed the instrumental virtuosity required by progressive rock, concentrating instead on flamboyant and outrageous stage antics and high energy, raucous music. They channelled the attitude of much of the nation into attacking their instruments in a raw, uncompromising way. These bands directly influenced British punk bands such as The Sex Pistols, The Clash, The Buzzcocks and The Damned. The Ramones were their contemporaries in the US, releasing their first album just before any of the British acts.

Punk bands used their guitars almost as weapons into which they poured all their angst, anger and frustration. You do not need to be a talented musician to play punk music – attitude is the key factor. The instrumentation for a punk band was typically drumkit, bass, two electric guitars and raspy, shouted vocal. The guitars were played extremely aggressively and the guitarist would generally try to get as much distortion and feedback as possible. Punk guitarists were not tidy players – they revelled in noise making. There were no long solos – any solos tended to be repetitions of the vocal line or thrashing through the chord sequence another time. At the end of 1976, The Sex Pistols released their first single, 'Anarchy in the UK'. This was to be the definitive song of the style. The Sex Pistols' antics gained them immediate public attention, such as gratuitous swearing on a prime-time TV interview and their provocative dress style. Punks sported dyed hair spiked into enormous Mohican styles and multiple body piercings, as well as wearing chains, safety pins and torn clothing. Punks revelled in causing public outrage and behaved in a manner calculated to offend, or to at least challenge the status quo.

Punk music was an important release of a pressure valve, both in terms of the social context of the time and as a reaction to bloated musical styles that were inaccessible for young bands. It was destined to have a short lifespan due to its self-destructive nature. Punk bands fought amongst themselves as well as fighting against the establishment and many split up by the start of the 1980s.

The immediate influence of punk was to encourage less talented musicians that it was all right to have a go at making music, even if they were incapable of soloing like the big rock acts of the time. It spawned a whole new era of experimentation where people would look for ways to express themselves with some of the rawness of punk, but not necessarily the attitude. New Wave music fell into this category – a slightly less raw sound than punk, but still containing powerful, simple guitar lines. New wave bands tend to have less aggressive vocal lines than punk with more emphasis on the melody and lyrics. It became popular on both sides of the Atlantic – in the US with bands such as the B-52s and Talking Heads and in the UK with XTC and Elvis Costello. U2 had elements of new wave in their early music – the Edge's chiming, insistent guitar playing along with Bono's thoughtful lyrics and more tuneful style, but still delivered in a rather challenging way (for example 'I Will Follow' from their first album, *Boy*).

In the US, another style emerged, moving in the opposite direction to new wave. Hardcore was a more intense version of punk – punk played at a higher tempo with even more uncompromising guitar sounds. The most famous hardcore band was the Dead Kennedys.

Indie rock

In Britain in the early 1980s, the major record labels and acts signed to them dominated British pop music. Unless you were signed to one of these labels, it was very hard to break into the music industry. In London, a Cambridge graduate called Geoff Travis set up a record store, Rough Trade, that he dedicated to selling music made by local bands. He realised that he had found a niche in the market, but he had no means of distributing the material (this is why the major labels had the market cornered). He overcame this problem by contacting other like-minded record shops around the country, setting up an independent distribution network. The project was not financially viable from the perspective of a multi-national, corporate label, but people like Travis were doing this primarily for the love of the music, not the financial rewards. Gradually, as more and more bands flocked to Travis and his independent distribution system, his record shop became a record label, independent of the major labels, so acts involved with him were called 'Indie' bands. Artists signed to Travis' label tended to be on significantly better deals than they would have had with a major label, but for them the important thing was that they kept ownership of their own music – something a major label would not have allowed.

A similar situation was occurring in Manchester where Tony Wilson was setting up a label, Factory Records, with the primary purpose of distributing the work of a band called Joy Division. Using this simple distribution principle, Joy Division managed to achieve nationwide recognition. Joy Division were heavily influenced by the Velvet Underground and the punk movement in general.

In 1982, Johnny Marr and Morrissey formed The Smiths. They were influenced by 1960s rock music and the punk and new wave scene, rejecting the synth-based pop sound of the 1980s for a chiming, guitar-driven sound reminiscent of bands like the Byrds. Morrissey's lyrics were full of dark humour and sarcasm, with Marr's guitar the perfect counterpoint for his vocal delivery. Marr tuned his guitar up a full tone to suit Morrissey's vocal range and to achieve a more 'chiming' sound. They were anti-Thatcher, proud of the fact they were English and espoused the indie 'right-on' attitude. Their mode of dress was almost as if they had walked in off the street, but that was the point – they were trying to get away from the spandex and big hair of the overblown, over-styled 1980s acts in the charts. The Smiths influenced many bands to come after them, including the Britpop bands of the 1990s.

Club dance

Disco came about in the mid-1970s as a fusion of the Philly soul sound with the rhythms of funk. Originally it was mainly a feature of the gay clubs, but it gradually made its way into the mainstream, bursting into the public imagination with the release of the film 'Saturday Night Fever'. Producers were very important in disco music, with Giorgio Moroder and Tom Moulton perhaps the most famous. Moroder worked closely with Donna Summer on a number of her biggest disco hits, including the classic 'I Feel Love'. Other disco artists included the Bee Gees and the Jacksons.

In the early to mid-1980s, Frankie Knuckles was DJing in the Warehouse Club, Chicago. He played a mixture of disco hits, soul and funk, adding a Roland TR-909 drum machine to his mixes to fatten the four-to-the-floor bass drum on the disco tracks. In order to keep his audience interested, he started to remix the tracks he owned, adding some extra sounds to the original tracks and mixing them together. As the music developed, he began to use more and more of his own beats on top of which he could add some of his standard playlist material. The style he developed was named after the club he worked in – 'House' music. It had the exaggerated four-to-the-floor beat and a sparse texture.

House music became popular in the UK and, with the addition of the Roland TB-303, it morphed into a new style called 'acid house', apparently named after the squelchy sound of the TB-303 bass timbre (and not after the drug LSD, although many would argue that it is…). Acid house music became very popular in the UK rave scene. The raves would attract drug dealing, so they were made illegal in England. However, the organisers would start to arrange them at venues dotted around the M25 outside London, avoiding the authorities.

DJ Larry Levan took influences from soul rather than R&B, mixing a more melodic form of music than the sparse 'house' music in his club in New York called the Paradise Garage. The music he mixed gradually became known as 'garage' music. Garage also made a quick trans-Atlantic journey and became very popular in London clubs such as the Ministry of Sound. Garage music, being based more on soul, was much more melodic than house music.

Other styles of club dance music:

- Techno
- Trance
- Jungle/Drum and bass
- Trip hop
- Goa
- Hard house.

There are many genres and sub-genres of club dance music, with the list growing every day. For the purposes of GCE Music Technology it is sufficient to learn about the main styles listed above and how they inter-relate.

Exam technique and practical issues

- Preparing equipment
- Exam technique.

Preparing equipment

Before you sit your exam you should be familiar with the CD player you are going to use and check that the headphones work as you expect. There may be an audio announcement at the start of the CD to check the orientation of the headphones ('left channel… right channel … left channel … right channel', where the voice comes out of the appropriate speaker as it is spoken), but in the absence of this, you should be confident that your headphones work as expected (including playback of the full audible frequency range without significant colouration at any one point in the range). The CD player will need to have the facility to fast forward and rewind in addition to skip forward and backwards or you will be put at a disadvantage. It is acceptable to use the CD-ROM drive of a computer for this purpose, but you are not allowed to make use of any sequencing software – just the media player required to allow access to the transport controls of the CD drive. It is a good idea to check the specific equipment you will be using in advance of the exam itself, just to put your mind at ease.

Exam technique

To achieve the best possible results in any exam, it is not enough just to know all the answers, you must know how to communicate them to the examiner and how to approach the paper itself. These are the four important elements in the successful completion of unit 2:

- Time management
- Use of the CD
- What does the question ask?
- How should I present the answer?

Time management

1. There are six questions in the exam, but they are not equally weighted.
2. Section A and section B are worth 40 marks each, so you should spend approximately 50 minutes completing each section.
3. Section A has 4 questions, so they should take just over 10 minutes each.
4. Section B has 2 questions, so they should take approximately 25 minutes each.
5. As a general rule of thumb, if there are 80 marks available in the whole paper, you should spend no more than 5 minutes for every 4 marks available. This will give you a little slack for particularly challenging or time-consuming questions.

Use of the CD

1. The CD will probably contain the complete songs used in each question, but you do not have time to listen through the songs aimlessly.
2. Read the question to see what part of the song it is referring to and skip straight to that point in the song, pausing the CD after the relevant section has ended
3. If the technology allows, set up an A–B loop so you can listen over and over to the relevant piece of audio without having to find the starting point afresh each time.
4. When you are answering a question that does not refer directly to the audio, stop the CD – it may adversely influence your response.
5. Do not listen through to the end of the track unless the question demands it.

What does the question ask?

1. Read the question carefully.
2. Read the question carefully again, underlining the important words.
3. Ensure you are answering exactly what is asked – you are listening to the right instrument being played at the right point in the right song. If the question demands a longer response, is the information you are putting down directly answering what is asked?
4. Check the amount of marks awarded for your response. Have you given enough individual points to merit the maximum marks?
5. If the answer is in table form, does it ask for comparative language or do you just have to make statements?

How should I present the answer?

1. For multiple choice questions, check that you have ticked the correct amount of boxes. If you make an error, ensure that the correction is clearly indicated (as instructed on the front of the exam paper).
2. Present your work clearly and legibly. If you have to continue your work outside the space provided, ensure that you indicate

that you are doing so inside the space provided, clearly pointing to where the rest of your answer is. It is best to restrict yourself to the space provided – it has been limited to this size for a reason.

3. Unless prose is specifically asked for, it is acceptable to answer in list form or bullet points. Examiners hate waffle.

4. Justify any statements you make in longer responses. Use technical or musical vocabulary as appropriate, but do not use a word unless you are sure of its meaning.

5. When answering the context questions in section B, stick to the points asked for in the question – you don't have space or time to give lots of background information that isn't asked for.

Well done: you have now completed the AS course – time for A2!

Progression from Music Technology Portfolio 1

Many of the skills you needed to complete the AS course will be developed further for the A2 course. This section will highlight any additional skills, or any refinements required in your approach to the tasks from what was required for unit 1. Much of what you did for unit 1 is similar in unit 3 (although a higher standard is expected), so you will be referred back to the unit 1 chapter from time to time in order to avoid excess repetition. Some activities, while perfectly acceptable at AS level, are felt to be more appropriate for A2 level, so they are dealt with in this section.

Edexcel has tried to keep the mark schemes for the A2 tasks the same as those for the AS tasks when at all possible – so the weightings for different sections have only changed when a new element has been introduced to the task (for example, the live vocal track demands a new section in the mark scheme for task 3A). The exact wording has also been retained where possible. In fact, the mark scheme for task 3B is exactly the same as that for task 1B, so there is no need to include a new paraphrased version in this section – any differences in expectations are listed instead of repeating the information from the 1B section.

Task 3C is the task which differs the most from the corresponding AS task, so this is dealt with in more depth.

You need to be aware of the additional expectations at A2 level – even if the mark scheme uses exactly the same words, a more polished, professional response is expected at A2 than at AS level. Treat all the tasks as if you are an industry professional, dependent on your client being happy enough with the quality of your work to book you again or to recommend you to other potential clients.

What does the task entail?

As for task 1A, the sequenced integrated performance requires you to listen to an original track and to recreate every detail of the track in your sequence. The big difference between the two tasks is that you must now record the lead vocal part as a live audio track **instead** of sequencing it. You do not need to sequence the lead vocal part with a suitable timbre – you need to record the live audio and mix it with your sequenced tracks so that it sits well with the other tracks, forming part of a whole rather than sounding like vocal + backing track.

The stimulus material will be provided by Edexcel in the September of your A2 year. This will consist of a choice of two tracks, but no skeleton score will be provided. You will be expected to work out all the parts under your own steam.

It is possible to record one or two audio tracks **in addition** to the vocal track – a maximum of two additional audio tracks is acceptable with any more attracting penalties. Thus, if you deemed it necessary, you could record three audio tracks in total – the lead vocal and two additional audio tracks. This may be useful depending on the stimulus material and on your particular areas of expertise. For example, if there is an acoustic guitar part in the stimulus it will take much less time to record it live than to try and produce an authentic-sounding sequence. You may also wish to record backing vocal parts instead of finding suitable timbres to represent these in your sequence.

Progression from task 1A to task 3A – what has stayed the same?

The rules for completing the task are the same as for task 1A – the work must be completed under controlled conditions with the distinction between preparation and writing time remaining the same (although there are a few aspects which are slightly different due to the additional audio recording required – see the 'what is different' paragraph below), the writing time allowance of 20 hours is the same, the same sound sources are permitted and so on.

Similarities between tasks 1A and 3A:

> The golden rule for this task, as with task 1A is – you should copy the original audio track in every possible detail.

- ○ A sequence replicating a stimulus song in every possible detail
- ○ Sound sources for the sequence may include GM (General MIDI) sounds, software instruments, virtual sound modules, sound cards, sound modules, sample libraries (providing individual hits) and samples only as specified by Edexcel on the stimulus material
- ○ The task must be completed under controlled conditions
- ○ The task is split into activities listed under 'preparation time' and those under 'writing time'
- ○ Any work done to the file that will eventually be mixed down into a stereo track for submission to the examiner is considered to be 'writing time'. See task 1A (pages 9–10) for a list of activities considered as preparation
- ○ All work considered as 'writing time' must be completed within a maximum time limit of 20 hours
- ○ The sequence must be mixed down to a final stereo file which is transferred to CD as track 1 of the music technology portfolio.

Another aspect of task 1A to carry over into task 3A is how you budget your time. With the exception of the audio track(s), all the parts must be sequenced in the same way as for task 1A, so refer to the section on completing the sequencing task (page 12) for help with this.

Progression from task 1A to task 3A – what is different?

Differences between tasks 1A and 3A	
Task 1A – Sequenced Realised Performance	Task 3A – Sequenced Integrated Performance
One stimulus track – no choice	Choice of two stimulus tracks
Skeleton score provided	No score provided
All the parts must be sequenced	The lead vocal must be a live, recorded vocal performance (with an optional one or two additional audio tracks)

Choice of stimulus tracks

In task 1A there was only one possible stimulus song that could be sequenced – no choice was offered. For task 3A a live vocal part has to be recorded in addition to the sequenced parts – this places different demands on resources (for example, a female vocalist may not be available in a boys' school), so a choice of two stimulus songs is offered. You should choose the song that best suits the vocalists you have available – this should be the main driving factor in your choice. If you have a range of vocalists available who would be equally comfortable singing either of the stimulus songs, you should choose whichever song will most motivate you to put in the necessary time and effort.

No score provided

There is no skeleton score provided for either stimulus in task 3A. This does not necessarily mean that you have to complete every aspect of the transcription process by ear – there are no marks for the transcription process itself, just for the accuracy of data input. It is still a good idea to transcribe as much as possible of the song by ear, if just for the discipline of the process, but you may use other resources to assist you, such as existing professional scores of the track. If you do use an external source to assist in the transcription process you need to be aware that it may not be exactly accurate to the recording (for example, some internet guitar tabs are very inaccurate) – elements such as slight developments in the melody, or an altered chord during a repeat are often overlooked, even in professional scores, so be wary. Remember – your ear is king. If it doesn't sound right then it probably isn't – locate the error and correct it so that it sounds like the original audio. The original audio is always the standard by which accuracy is judged, not any printed score.

Integration of live audio

The biggest difference between this task and task 1A is the integration of live audio. This also poses the biggest challenges and is the aspect you should take most care with. You must record the lead vocal part as a live recording and integrate it with the sequenced tracks so that it sounds like it belongs in the recording rather than sitting rather uncomfortably on top of a MIDI backing track. There are some tricks you can use to secure the greatest chances of success at this, which we shall go into later.

What is the examiner looking for?

The examiner wants to hear a piece of music that is as close as possible to the original stimulus song in every detail.

Note that the weighting for criterion 1: accuracy of note input is now four marks less to allow for the extra four marks in criterion 4: music technology skills. The section on the quality of the recording has now been replaced by 'capture of live audio'.

1. Accuracy of note input

Pitch	6	Completely accurate. The sequence sounds just like the original track. There are no pitch errors at all.
	4 – 5	There may be a few pitch errors in the sequence, but the piece still sounds good. This category is used when there are errors, but they are tricky to spot.
	3	When there are more obvious errors that can easily be spotted or if there are repeated errors (such as a section which has been copied and pasted, but the original was wrong or an accidental has been consistently missed) the piece will fall into this category.
	2	When the errors start to make you cringe then the sequence will fall into this category.
	1	When only some of the track is accurate – there are more errors than there are correct notes, or there are sections of the piece that contain some very serious pitch problems.
Rhythm	6	Completely accurate. The sequence sounds just like the original track. There are no errors in rhythm input at all **and** the track sounds musical – there is a human feel to it rather than all the notes falling on the grid lines.
	4 – 5	The piece may be 100% accurate, but it feels a bit mechanical and unmusical: 5 marks. A few errors in the rhythm input, but these are quite hard to spot – they don't take anything away from the sequence.
	3	Errors are quite easily spotted, but the piece still sounds OK. If the different parts feel like they are playing out of time with each other then the sequence will fall into this category.
	2	Rhythmic errors make the sequence sound unmusical. There may be some serious errors that are repeated a lot (e.g. a repeated drum loop is wrong throughout in addition to some other rhythmic problems).
	1	When only some parts are accurate – there are problems in all or most parts.

> Note that this section refers only to the **sequenced** parts – it is not assessing the accuracy of the live recorded track(s).
>
> As with task 1A, if there are parts missing from the sequence the examiner will take a percentage off the final mark. **Do not** leave tracks out.

2. Choice and mix of sounds

Timbre	4	All the chosen sounds are very close to those used in the original track. Presets have been edited in some way to make them sound more like the original track. **Note:** You can only score 4 marks if there has been some editing of the preset sounds (refer to this in your log).
	3	All the chosen sounds are very close to those in the original track but there has been no editing of preset timbres. Or, there is some editing of presets, but there is the odd dodgy choice of timbre.
	2	Most of the sounds chosen are good, but there is the odd dodgy choice. If an inappropriate live instrument has been chosen to replace one of the parts from the stimulus the sequence will fall into this category.
	1	There are several poor choices of timbre **or** the timbres chosen are in the same sort of family, but they sound nothing like those on the original track (for example, synths have been chosen for the synth tracks, but they just don't come close to sounding like the original).
Balance and Pan	4	All the parts have been balanced and panned just like they are in the original track (including any odd balancing or panning in the original). The audio tracks blend well with the sequenced tracks – they don't stand out as being 'different' to the sequenced tracks.
	3	The balance and panning are good, but may be different from the stimulus. The audio tracks generally sit well in the mix, although overall it doesn't quite give the impression that everything belongs together in the mix.
	2	There are some important parts that can't be clearly heard (for example, some solo parts are too quiet or some background parts are too loud) and/or some of the parts have not been panned properly. The audio tracks sit a little uncomfortably on top of the sequenced tracks.
	1	There are several problems with the balance that make the sequence sound muddy or unclear and/or none of the parts have been panned. The audio tracks feel completely separate to the sequenced tracks.

Timbre refers to the choice of sounds for the sequenced parts, but if you have chosen to replace more than the vocal track with live audio, this may come into play here too.

Balance and pan is marked according to the whole mix, not just the sequenced tracks.

3. Musicality

Dynamics	4	The dynamics are a faithful reproduction of the original and include volume swells etc. during notes (dynamic shaping) in addition to velocity changes.
	3	The main dynamic contrasts are present in the piece, but there are not many examples of dynamic shaping or there is a good deal of dynamic shaping etc., but it is not faithful to the original.
	2	It is clear that there has been some attempt to recreate the dynamics of the original, but there are some places where they are unsuccessful (for example, crescs and dims are too sudden or grainy or too extreme).
	1	There has been some attempt to input dynamics, but most of those that have been programmed are either too subtle to have any effect or are unmusical (perhaps because they are too extreme or 'lumpy').
Articulation and Phrasing	4	The parts have been programmed so that they sound musical – the articulation and phrasing makes it sound like live musicians have performed them. Any of the obvious staccatos/legatos/tail-offs at the ends of phrases etc. of the original have been convincingly recreated in the sequence.
	3	Most of the phrasing of the original has been attempted but it is not entirely convincing or there is some musical phrasing and articulation, but it does not relate to the original track.
	2	There are clear attempts to edit the length, start times and relative strength of notes to create phrasing and articulation, but it sounds a little robotic.
	1	There has been little attempt to include any aspects of phrasing or articulation. Any attempts are either overly mechanical or actually take away from the success of the sequence (for example, frequent evidence of very short staccato, notes audibly overlapping or unmusical pitch-bends).

This section is assessed on the sequenced tracks only. The dynamic contrasts and articulation/phrasing in the live, recorded audio parts are not dealt with here.

4. Music Technology Skills

Style and Creativity	4	A musical sequence. Any particular challenges posed by the stimulus material have been met. FX are appropriate and add to the piece. There is convincing use of pitch bend, modulation etc. to recreate elements of the original. Any tempo shaping adds to the piece. There is a feeling that the style of the original has been captured in the sequence.
	3	A consistent sense of style with some attention to musical detail resulting in a generally successful sequence.
	2	Where tempo shaping has been used, there may be one or two problems that have been introduced. FX have been used, but not always in a way that is suitable for the stimulus material. Some work has gone into editing the sequence, but it still doesn't really sound musical. A workmanlike attempt at making the piece sound like the original, but it hasn't quite hit the mark.
	1	The piece sounds quite robotic, with few obvious attempts to make it fit within the style. Any FX which are used are not really appropriate and, if tempo shaping has been used, it takes away from the success of the sequence rather than adding to it.
Capture of Live Audio	8	Mics have been well chosen for the task with the audio tracks captured clearly. No problems have arisen as a result of poor mic placement. There are no unwanted noises or hiss on the live, recorded tracks. The audio tracks have been EQed so that they can sit properly in the mix with an appropriate amount of compression used. Any processing used is appropriate to the style.
	6 – 7	The audio tracks have been generally well captured, but several of the requirements listed in the above level have not quite been met.
	4 – 5	The mic choice is mostly good. There may be one audio track that has not been captured so well or where mic placement has caused other issues. There is a little noise present in one of the audio tracks, but it is not terribly noticeable. One or more of the tracks could have done with a little more attention to EQ and/or dynamics to help it gel with the sequenced tracks.
	2 – 3	The mic choice and/or positioning has caused problems for the capture of the live audio. There is some noticeable noise present on one or more of the audio tracks. There are some peaks in the frequency range that have not been ironed out and/or the lack of dynamics processing causes the live track(s) to leap out of the mix on occasion.
	1	Poor mic choice and placement. A noisy recording in most areas. No EQ or dynamics processing have been used or, where they are used, they take away from the quality of the recording rather than add to it.

Any effects added to the live audio will help it to sit well in the mix, so will gain credit in criterion 2: 'choice and mix of sounds' as well as under 'style and creativity' as it may be very difficult to separate out what reverb has been applied to the sequenced parts and what has been applied to the live tracks. The capture and processing of the sounds is assessed in 'criterion 4: music technology skills'.

The 'capture of live audio' section looks at several aspects of the recording quality, so it is unlikely that all of these aspects will do exactly what any one level in the mark scheme suggests they should. Here you should apply a 'best-fit' approach to the mark scheme, underlining any statements that are true of the recorded audio tracks in each of the different areas (mic choice and placement, capture, elimination of noise, EQ and dynamics). Some areas may fall in the 2–3 level while others may be in the top level. The actual mark for this section will be a resultant average of all these areas.

Completing the sequenced integrated performance

Much of the detail related to skills and techniques required for this section has been covered already in tasks 1A and 1B, so this section will refer back to these as appropriate. This section is intended more as a checklist to ensure that you attempt task 3A in an efficient way, maximising your use of the 20 hours allowed for writing time and making the most of your own resources and those of your vocalist and musicians. You should attempt the task in the following order:

○ Preparation (1) – stimulus choice, transcription, learning and practising parts
○ Data input
○ Editing of sequenced parts
○ Basic mix
○ Preparation (2) – Rehearsing live parts, preparing for session
○ Record live parts
○ Process live parts and mixing
○ Completing the logbook.

Preparation (1)

Stimulus choice

The first thing you need to decide on is which of the two stimuli provided by Edexcel is the most suitable for you and your resources. The choice should be determined by the following factors (in order of importance).

1. Available vocalist(s) – if you don't have anyone who can sing one of the songs then your choice is made for you straight away. If you don't have anyone available to sing either of the stimuli then you will need to take further steps (see the section on rehearsing the live parts, page 108).
2. Play to the strengths of your equipment – one stimulus will suit the available equipment more than the other in terms of choice of sounds, style of music and so on.
3. Which of the two stimuli will motivate you to work hard for a prolonged period of time?
4. Is there anything in one of the two stimuli that you will find particularly difficult or is there another reason for not choosing it?

Transcription

A skeleton score is not provided by Edexcel for this task, so you will have to transcribe all the parts yourself. There may be a score commercially available for your chosen stimulus and there will certainly be a piano reduction available somewhere. It is acceptable to use these as starting points for your transcription, but be aware that Edexcel have not endorsed any of these as being 100% accurate – it is entirely up to you to determine how accurate any given score is to the stimulus audio. **Remember – the audio track is what you must copy, not any particular score.**

See page 13 for more details of how to go about transcribing the stimulus song.

At this point you should make decisions about what, if any, additional audio tracks you are going to include. You have the option of recording up to two more live audio tracks as well as the live vocal, so you may wish to lessen the sequencing requirement by accepting this offer. The downside of this is that you have more audio tracks to 'smooth' into the mix and more opportunity for losing marks in the 'capture of live audio' criterion, but additional audio parts may help to make the whole task seem a little more together. Your decisions should be based on your available resources including the relative strengths of MIDI sounds and availability of live performers. If there are four backing vocal tracks, it would sound odd to record two of these as live and two as MIDI, so keep your choices logical.

Learning and practising parts

Your keyboard skills will hopefully have improved since the beginning of the AS course, so you should now be able to input at least part of the sequence by playing it in on a MIDI keyboard. You should decide which parts will benefit the most from being played in live and which parts will actually be better input using a mouse (by making judgements on which parts sound most mechanical or programmed in the original stimulus song). Practise any of the parts you intend to play in live, perhaps practising them in small chunks for later input during the writing time.

Data input

As soon as data input begins, the clock starts for the 20 hours writing time (meaning you must be completing this section under controlled conditions). Be aware that this task will take more time in some areas and less time in others than task 1A did, so do not expect to be at exactly the same place at the same point into your writing time. You do not have to input the lead vocal part, so this may mean you will take significantly less time at this stage of the process, depending on how you went about things in task 1A. Remember that you can do more preparation work at any point – you do not have to complete all 20 hours of writing time consecutively.

Editing of sequenced parts

The sequenced parts should be edited in exactly the same way as you did for task 1A. The mark scheme is almost identical for this element of the task, but you will be expected to make things sound a little more musical than was the case at AS level – try to introduce an extra layer of polish. You know what worked and what didn't work for you when you tried this before, so the experience will help you to execute this part of the task much quicker.

Basic mix

After entering and editing the sequenced parts, you should do a basic mix so that the live performers have something they can react to when they record their parts. Add some provisional effects to help the sequence sound more impressive, although you will probably change the reverb settings after the live audio is recorded. If the sequenced parts sound lifeless, it is going to be difficult to get a great performance out of your live musicians, so the more time you spend getting things right before you record, the better for the final product.

Preparation (2)

Rehearsing live parts

Give each of your performers an audio CD of the sequenced 'backing' so they can practise their parts to the actual sound they will hear while recording. Check with your teacher before you do this, because you do not want to contravene controlled conditions. If you do give someone a CD, it MUST be a finalised stereo audio track rather than the sequence file. To do otherwise may have severe consequences. If there are problems with this, depending on the way your centre is administering the day-to-day running of controlled conditions, it should be possible to rehearse your performers along to the sequencer in your presence – this rehearsal will still count towards preparation time rather than writing time.

Preparing for session

Refer to page 40 for more details on session planning, checking equipment, considering acoustics and setting up equipment. All of these elements still fall under preparation time, so may be completed under limited supervision. As with task 1B, your teacher must supervise your final microphone placement, even though this is still technically preparation time.

Record live parts

Refer to the sections on microphone placement for tasks 1B (page 49) and 3B (page 114, drum kit only), for more details on the capture of live audio.

Processing live parts and mixing

The most difficult part of the task and the one that may be most fundamental to its success is the processing of the live audio parts. It is difficult to make live parts sit well with sequenced parts simply because the sequenced parts are all pre-processed synth timbres that have generally been compressed to within an inch of their lives and have had all sorts of impressive effects added in order to make them sound good as you browse through the presets in a music shop. So one part of this process might be not just to process your live sounds effectively, but to thin out some of the synth timbres in order to leave some space for the live sounds. If you are happy with the accuracy and editing for musicality of the sequenced parts, it is possible to export each track individually as audio and process them in the audio domain along with the live tracks – this will allow you to use the same effects on both the sequenced parts and the live parts, so may assist in getting a more 'together', homogenous sound. It may be necessary to subtly EQ some of the sequenced parts in the frequency range dominated by the live parts so that they don't fight for space.

You will need to compress the live parts, and sometimes you will need to apply compression twice to a track (or two compressors in series) to get the desired effect. Be careful with the settings here – you can easily make the compressor act as a glorified volume control if you don't take care with the threshold and ratio settings in particular. A compressor setting with a relatively high ratio (say, 5:1) effecting only the peaks of the signal (a high threshold setting) followed by a much more gentle ratio (as low as 1.5:1 or less) with a much lower threshold setting will help even the more extreme dynamics to be tamed somewhat, but be careful that you do not introduce unwanted artefacts (such as a 'pumping' characteristic) unless this is something you can hear in the original recording. Another thing to be aware of is that the compressor will raise the volume of all the lower levels relative to the higher levels – this includes any background hiss, so edit the audio carefully, trimming 'silences' at the beginnings and endings of phrases before you apply a lot of compression.

Analyse the stimulus song and identify what sort of effects and processing are being used on each track. Unlike tasks 1B and 3B, you must try and replicate what you hear as closely as possible, so experiment with the effects units at your disposal to see if you can find similar settings to those on the original song. Edit these as appropriate so as to get as close as possible to the original and apply to the individual tracks in your sequenced integrated performance as appropriate.

Ensure that the balance and panning settings of your mix are as close as possible to the original track, even if you feel that some of the original settings could be improved.

Constantly compare your work to the original track. It is a good idea to keep several copies of your work, so that you can go back to a previous version if you experiment with various mixing techniques and later decide to abandon them – it will save a lot of undoing.

As with any audio mix, after you have finished it, leave it for a while (at least two or three days) and then return to listen with fresh ears. Also, try to listen to the final mix (on finalised audio CD) on as many stereo systems as is feasible (again, check with your teacher before removing anything from controlled conditions).

Completing the logbook

The logbook for Music Technology Portfolio 2 does not attract any marks in itself – all your marks are awarded on the basis of the audio you present to the examiner on your final CD. However, the logbook is a valuable method of recording any important information you wish to draw to the examiner's attention, particularly in the editing of timbres and effects, that may not be immediately obvious. Questions 1–3 of the logbook refer to the sequenced integrated performance and are mostly asking you to list the equipment used (and the source of any samples if this is allowed in the year of your examination). Feel free to add information you feel is valuable, but keep it concise.

What does the task entail?

As for task 1B, you are expected to produce a recording of the highest possible quality. The only real difference between task 1B and 3B is the introduction of a recording topic and slightly increased requirements in the length of recording and track count.

Progression from task 1B to task 3B – what is different?

Progression from task 1B to task 3B - differences	
Task 1B – Multi-track recording	Task 3B – Multi-track recording
Lasts between 2 and 4 minutes	Lasts between 3 and 5 minutes
Minimum of 8 tracks	Minimum of 12 tracks
Minimum of 4 tracks captured using microphones	Minimum of 8 tracks captured using microphones
No recording topic	Choice of recording topic A or B
Free selection of stimulus material from Area of Study 2: Popular Music Styles since 1910	Free selection of stimulus material from Area of Study 3: The Development of Technology-based Music

Specification requirements

The recording should be completed under controlled conditions, with exactly the same elements falling under the headings of preparation and writing time as for task 1B (see page 34 for details).

The recording should last no less than three minutes and no longer than five minutes. It is acceptable to alter the original song structure so that it fits within this timeframe.

There must be a minimum of 12 tracks in your recording. The method of working out track count is the same as for task 1B. The specification states that there should be a maximum of 24 tracks used, but you will not be penalised if you use more than 24 tracks in your recording. The maximum was included as a guide to discourage overly complex recordings that concentrate on quantity over quality. Of these 12 or more tracks, at least 8 should be captured using microphones. It is not necessary to use DI techniques if you do not deem them appropriate for your recording.

The recording must make use of overdubbing. It is acceptable to capture multiple instruments in one take, but you must overdub at least one more track afterwards.

Use of MIDI and loops/samples is prohibited in this task – you must only use live musicians.

The music you choose to record must be commercially available. It is not acceptable to record a song by your own band, even if you have released it commercially.

There appears to be a difference between tasks 1B and 3B in the option of the recording stimulus material, but in practice this does not make much difference at all. It is very difficult to separate the development of technology-based music from popular music styles since 1910 because so much of the development of music technology has been driven by the world of popular music. The only difference is that it would be possible to record music for task 3B that is from the art music world of experimental and electronic music, or any other style of music that makes use of music technology in addition to the obvious choices from popular music styles.

Recording Topics

Aside from the minor changes in minimum requirements, there is one additional factor to consider – the introduction of recording topics. The specification gives the choice of two topics:

Topic A: Recording acoustic and/or orchestral instruments
Topic B: Recording percussion instruments.

For topic A you are expected to 'use at least four acoustic and/or orchestral instruments'. The specification follows this with some slightly confusing wording that basically says you can combine these four acoustic/orchestral instruments with anything else you want.

For topic B you are expected to 'use at least four percussion instruments. These may be Latin, tuned, untuned, orchestral or world, but a standard drum set counts as one instrument.'

Have you spotted the slight issue here? For topic B you have to use four percussion instruments – but these are acoustic instruments in their own right! This means that the choice of topics is actually rather irrelevant since if you used four percussion instruments you could submit your recording for either topic A or B.

So, to summarise the additional specification requirement:

- ○ You must include at least four acoustic instruments in your multi-track recording. An acoustic instrument is one that doesn't plug into an amplifier. You can combine these with anything else including acoustic or electric instruments and/or voice(s).

What is the examiner looking for?

The mark schemes for task 1B and 3B are identical in the specification, so there is no need to repeat a paraphrased version here. Refer to page 31 for the paraphrased mark scheme. The only difference is that recordings at A2 level will be expected to be just that little bit more polished than was the case at AS level.

That little bit more polished...?

Although the mark scheme is the same, a slightly higher level of sophistication will be expected, especially in the processing section. For task 1B it is sufficient to make good use of a parametric EQ (or several) for management of EQ, compression for management of dynamics and reverb (and possibly delay) for effects/ambience. For task 3B you will be expected to understand, and make use of (as appropriate) enhancers, various forms of shelving and parametric EQ including the use of various EQ settings, filters, gates/expanders, limiters, various types of reverb, delay and modulation effects. As always, the overuse or misuse of effects is probably worse than not using them at all, so subtlety should reign supreme – the 'less is more' approach is generally the best. When you listen to impressive mixes, they can often sound deceptively simple, but the producer has probably included lots of different processors and effects in subtle ways to enhance every aspect of the sound throughout the track.

For the capture and mixing criteria, a 'little bit more polished' refers to the fact that you have to deal with more tracks, but still make them fit within a well-crafted mix, so the task itself demands more of you rather than the examiner expecting the mix to be somehow better – these sections will be marked in exactly the same way as the AS multi-track recording.

Completing the multi-track recording

The nature of the task is identical to that of task 1B – refer to task 1B page 30 for details of how to approach a multi-track recording.

As well as the slightly increased minimum requirements, there is the additional factor of the recording topics to take into consideration when choosing a stimulus. The recording topics demand that you record four acoustic instruments (which may be percussion instruments if you opt for topic B). This may cause problems when it comes to choosing an appropriate song to record. The points referring to stimulus choice on page 37 still hold true, but note particularly the last paragraph that discusses altering the instrumentation to suit the circumstances – this may be necessary in task 3B in order to meet the minimum requirements, otherwise everyone will probably have to choose Santana tracks to complete topic B! It is acceptable to add additional percussion to any existing instrumentation in order to meet the minimum requirements of topic B, but do make sure that they add to the sound rather than take away from it. Similarly, it is possible to include additional acoustic instruments (such as an extra trumpet or saxophone) in order to meet the requirements of topic A. One option is to replace a synth string pad sound that already exists in the stimulus track with a live string quartet – this will instantly fulfil the requirements, and will be much more interesting into the bargain!

It is not necessary for the four acoustic instruments to be playing all the way through the track – as long as they are present in reasonable doses they will be fulfilling the specification requirements, but you should exercise judgement as to how much or little you use them. If you used a triangle, clash cymbals, glockenspiel and orchestral bass drum for one note each in the entire recording, it would be felt that you were not following the spirit of the specification requirements and you would be penalised accordingly.

Recording the drum kit

Recording drums is one of the most challenging and satisfying aspects of the engineer's job. Every expert will have developed their own set of tricks, and slightly differing approaches in terms of microphone selection and placement, methods of dampening various parts of the kit, getting a good snare and kick sound, getting the most from hi-hats, getting the maximum 'zing' from cymbals and tuning toms and so on, so saying that there is one 'right' way to record a drum kit would be foolish. Rather, there are a set of guidelines you can follow and, armed with a good understanding of basic mic techniques, a general knowledge of the drum kit itself and some general recording and production skills, you can hone your abilities until you develop your own personal tricks for getting the best from a drum kit.

Before you start recording, check for any rattles, buzzes or other unwanted noises from the kit. Ask the drummer to play through the song you are about to record and listen carefully for any noises. Sometimes, the drums will make other objects in the room vibrate, so if there is buzzing, it may not be from the drum kit itself!

Are you happy with the sound of the kit? If you feel the toms are a bit resonant, you may wish to add some dampening to the skins or you may wish to tune them differently. If the drummer is using 'O-rings' as a way of dampening the toms, check that they aren't rattling against the skins. Has the bass drum sufficient dampening to give it the solid 'thud' sound you want? If not, you should push some material such as a blanket up against the skin. Is there enough definition in the kick drum sound? One trick you may wish to use it to tape some plastic (or simply a wad of gaffer tape) to either the beater head itself or to the skin where the beater strikes – this will generate a definite click sound, but it may be too much for your taste.

Typical multi-mic setup

Overhead view

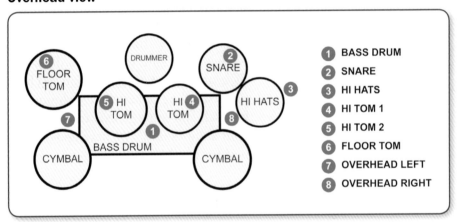

1	BASS DRUM	
2	SNARE	
3	HI HATS	
4	HI TOM 1	
5	HI TOM 2	
6	FLOOR TOM	
7	OVERHEAD LEFT	
8	OVERHEAD RIGHT	

The diagrams demonstrate an 8-mic setup. Generally, once you get beyond stereo overheads, kick and snare then you need to start putting a mic on each piece of the kit. This is where things get a little tricky. You need to get as close as possible to the drum heads without getting in the way of the drummer – especially if you are using individual mic stands for each mic, but you also need to think about the directional characteristics of the mics. There are drum mic sets available, but some of these contain hypercardioid response mics, so you need to be aware if you are using these, that there will be a significant response from the back of the mic as well as from the front. Experiment with the exact placement of the mic in relation to the skin, especially with the snare – you will get a different sound from very minor adjustments of the mic position. Dynamic mics will generally be best for the toms and snare, mostly because they are robust enough to withstand the drummer hitting them by accident.

Put the bass drum mic on an extendable, low boom mic stand. Position it inside the drum so it is between 5 and 10 cms away from where the beater hits the skin. You should experiment with placement of the bass drum mic, because small adjustments can make a big difference to the overtones that are picked up. The bass drum mic should be one built specifically for the purpose of recording a bass drum (such as the AKG D112), because it has to pick up very low frequencies, some high frequencies and be robust enough to withstand the high SPLs encountered inside a bass drum.

Keep the hi-hat mic slightly above and outside of the cymbal itself – if it is directly above the hi-hat you may get a 'sucking' sound as the air is pulled away from the mic by the hi-hat closing. You should use a condenser mic for the hi-hat so as to faithfully capture all the high frequencies it produces.

The position of the overhead mics is entirely down to experimentation. You may wish to start with them about 1m above the kit, positioned so they are capturing the whole kit evenly.

It is unwise to use gates while recording and, if you decide you must use compression while recording, use very little. You cannot remove these after the recording process.

You may wish to add additional room mics to your setup – a stereo pair, two or three metres away from the kit, so as to pick up the sound of the room and the kit as a whole.

Another commonly used trick is to mic both the top and bottom head of the snare (and toms). This is thought to give the sound that extra bit of bite and power. There is one thing you need to be very careful of though – phase cancellation.

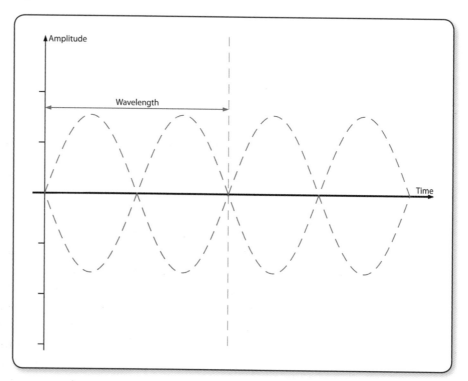

Back in chapter 1B we looked at a sine wave to explain how sound works. If you combine two sine waves, of equal amplitude and frequency, but that are exactly out of phase with each other then they will cancel each other out giving silence (as in the diagram above). Complete cancellation is unusual in real life, but cancellation of certain frequencies (particularly bass frequencies) is common. If you hit the snare drum, at that instant the top skin is moving downwards, 'sucking' the air away from the top mic while, at exactly the same instant, the bottom head is moving downwards too, 'pushing' the air towards the bottom mic. The two mics are 'seeing' the same drum sound, but exactly out of phase with each other, so they will exhibit phase cancellation. If you have a phase switch, then by pressing it for one of the microphone channels, you bring both mics into phase with each other again and you capture the sound you wanted.

Completing the logbook

Questions 4–7 of the logbook refer to task 3B, asking for details of the equipment used, how you setup the mics, the recording procedure and details about EQ, effects, dynamics processing, panning and mix level. Fill this in as thoroughly as possible, listing every detail of the effort you put into making your recording a success. If there is insufficient space on the track sheet supplied, photocopy a blank track sheet, fill in the additional tracks and insert the photocopy into the appropriate place in the logbook. It is often more informative to have photos rather than diagrams for the mic setup in question 5, so remember to bring a camera to the recording session to photograph the microphone placement.

The logbook does not attract any marks in itself, but be aware that your submission will not be marked unless you have completed the logbook and submitted it along with the audio CD for the music technology portfolio.

What does the task entail?

You are required to compose an original piece of music based on a brief you will choose from a selection of three published by Edexcel at the start of the A2 year. The briefs will offer the choice of composing:

1. Music for film or television
2. Electro-acoustic music
3. A popular song.

The briefs will specify how long your composition should be (normally three minutes, but never more than four minutes) and will also specify some conditions for the use of instruments, a theme or scenario to be played out in your composition, and possibly some structural elements (particularly for theme 1: music for film or television).

Progression from task 1C to task 3C – what has stayed the same?

The composing and arranging tasks both make use of your skills to creatively develop musical ideas, using music technology throughout the process in a creative way and also as a tool to help you realise and structure your ideas. Both mark schemes have a system where there are compulsory criteria on which every piece is judged and a set of optional criteria that are chosen according to the strengths of the piece.

Progression from task 1C to task 3C – what is different?

In the progression from AS to A2 level, the difference between task 1C and 3C is the most marked. Both use the same skills and similarly organised mark schemes, but the actual composing task is different from the arranging task in several respects:

Progression from task 1C to task 3C - differences

Task 1C – Creative Sequenced Arrangement	Task 3C – Composing Using Music Technology
Lasts between 2 and 3 minutes	Lasts between 3 and 4 minutes
Selection of stimulus song and styles provided	Selection of three briefs provided
Must be sequenced	Can contain any mix of music technology deemed appropriate to the composition
Arrangement must be based on stimulus material	Composition must be fundamentally original

The principle of task 3C is that you use any technology you see fit to produce an original piece of music that fulfils your selection from the three possible briefs. It does not have to be purely sequenced material (although it can be if you think this is appropriate), but can contain any number of samples and audio tracks as appropriate to the piece (unless otherwise specified by the brief).

In this task the brief is paramount. Always have it at the front of your mind as you come up with and manipulate your musical ideas. If anything written here or in any other documentation contradicts the brief, always go with what it says in the brief.

What is the examiner looking for?

The examiner wants to hear a coherent piece of music containing original and well-explored musical ideas that fulfils every aspect of the brief while making extensive use of music technology.

The first four criteria in the mark scheme are compulsory and are applied to every piece submitted, no matter what brief is chosen. Examiners will mark all compositions according to all five of the optional criteria and take forward the best three marks, ignoring the two weakest criteria.

Compulsory criteria (all assessed – 22 marks available):

1. Responding to set brief (6 marks)

2. Style/coherence (6 marks)

3. Manipulation of sounds (6 marks)

4. Quality of recorded submission (4 marks)

Optional criteria (best three marks counted – 18 marks available):

5. Melody (6 marks)

6. Harmony (6 marks)

7. Rhythm (6 marks)

8. Texture (6 marks)

9. Form/structure (6 marks)

1. Responding to Set Brief

6	The composition successfully fulfils all aspects of the brief, including attention to the instrumental resources used, the timings given and the mood created. It fulfils the brief in an imaginative way. A variety of technology has been used to compose and realise the piece.
4 – 5	Almost all aspects of the brief have been fulfilled, but there may be one area that is not quite met (e.g. the timings are slightly off in brief 1, the use of samples in brief 2 does not quite fulfil the requirements or the song doesn't use all the required instruments). However, the main aspects of the brief are clearly present in the composition.
2 – 3	Some elements of the brief have been fulfilled, but some have been ignored. The composition may be a little short (2'30" or less) or far too long (4'30" or more) for briefs 2 and 3. In the case of brief 1, the links between sections may be poor in addition to timings being incorrect.
1	Few, if any aspects of the brief have been observed. It feels as if this is a free composition. Any piece that lasts less than two minutes will fall into this category.

2. Style/Coherence

6	All parts of the composition feel as if they belong to one unified whole. The piece has a sense of direction at all times and the musical ideas have been developed in imaginative ways. The sense of style is consistent through all sections of the piece (or any intentional changes of style are wholly convincing).
4 – 5	The composition has a sense of style that is mostly consistent although there may be one or two ideas that don't feel as if they fully belong there. The piece has a sense of direction and the musical ideas have been developed. The parts of the composition feel as if they belong together, but there are the odd moments when the piece feels a little samey or as if there is slightly too much contrast.
2 – 3	The composition has a sense of style, but this is not always coherent – the style seems to change from time to time without sufficient reason to do so. There is sometimes not enough development of musical ideas – the ideas have been repeated, sometimes in different contexts, but they don't actually develop enough. The piece may feel a bit repetitive or there is too much contrast between the different sections resulting in a lack of flow from one section to the next.
1	There is little sense of style in the composition, or too many different styles are jostling for attention. Musical ideas are not really developed, even though they may be repeated many times. The different sections of the piece do not hang together well at all or the piece is exceedingly repetitive.

3. Manipulation of Sounds

6	Music technology has been used to manipulate sounds in imaginative ways, making full use of the available equipment. The resultant sounds are interesting and original, but still work well with the other sounds.
4 – 5	Music technology has been used to manipulate and shape some sounds in a way that works within the style of the composition. The sound shaping may not be totally original, but it works well in the context of the composition.
2 – 3	Sonic mangling distracts from the important elements of the composition **or** there is some manipulation of sounds, but it is a little restricted/very predictable.
1	There is little use of music technology to manipulate the sounds used in the composition **or** any sound manipulation that is used does not work in the context of the piece.

4. Quality of Recorded Submission

4	The final stereo recording has no blemishes in any way. The recording level is high without distorting and there is no evidence of clicks, hiss or clipping at any point in the track.
3	There are one or two small blemishes in the final audio recording: e.g., it clips once or twice, there is a little hiss audible during silences or the playout is slightly too long. However, the recording is still good quality.
2	There are several issues that take away from the success of the final recording: for example, the beginning or ending may be chopped, there may be noticeable hiss throughout or it may distort occasionally.
1	The final audio track is of poor quality. There may be a very long playout or a long silence at the beginning of the track or it may be mastered at a very low level.

Parts 3 and 4 of the mark scheme both refer to the use of music technology and are worth 10 marks in total, in keeping with the 10 marks available for use of music technology in task 1C.

5. Melody

6	The melodies sound stylish. They are imaginative and memorable. They have a good shape, flowing nicely (if appropriate to the style). There is clear evidence of melodic development throughout the composition.
4 – 5	Melodies have a sense of shape and work well – they are quite stylish. There is evidence of effective melodic development in the piece.
2 – 3	There are some awkward points in the melodies – they do not always seem to flow. There may be some awkward intervals or they sound stilted. There is some development of melodic ideas.
1	Melodies do not flow. They do not sound stylish. They are awkward and difficult to perform. There is no melodic development.

6. Harmony

6	There is an imaginative use of harmony/tonality in keeping with the style of the composition. The chosen harmonies do not clash with the melody in any way (unless clashes are clearly demanded by the style).
4 – 5	The harmonies work throughout the piece, with perhaps the odd, insignificant clash. They are consistent with the style of the composition.
2 – 3	There are some clashes in the harmony or the harmonies are dull and uninteresting. There are some awkward moments where the harmony doesn't quite fit with the melody.
1	The harmonies frequently clash with the melodic material. There has been little attempt to harmonise any melodic material or, where harmonies exist, they take away from the success of the composition rather than add to it.

7. Rhythm

6	Rhythm is central to the success of the composition. The rhythmic parts all work together well, either capturing an existing groove, or creating a new, original feel. The rhythms have been developed over the course of the composition.
4 – 5	The rhythmic parts work well in the composition, adding to its success. There is some development of the rhythmic material in the composition.
2 – 3	The rhythms mostly work in the composition, but they may sound a little unstylish or stilted. There is little development of rhythmic material. The composition may have a boring, overly repetitive rhythm or far too many rhythmic ideas jostling for attention.
1	The choice of rhythmic material is not appropriate for the style of the composition. There is no development of rhythmic material.

8. Texture

6	The texture is interesting and imaginative including appropriate contrasts at the right times. The choice and combination of timbres/instruments works well and is sufficiently varied throughout the piece to create an interesting texture.
4 – 5	Textural contrasts add interest to the piece. The choice of instruments is mostly appropriate and stylish, although there may be one or two choices that don't sit quite so comfortably.
2 – 3	The texture may remain too similar throughout or there may be some odd textural contrasts that don't really work. Some of the choices of instrument/timbre are unsuccessful.
1	There are many odd choices of timbres/instruments in the piece that do not work well. There is no textural contrast or there are several serious misjudgements in the use of textural contrast.

9. Form/Structure

6	Excellent and imaginative organisation of musical ideas.
4 – 5	Musical ideas are presented with a sense of direction and coherence as appropriate to the style with few misjudgements.
2 – 3	Some misjudgements in the organisation of musical ideas. May be excessively unpredictable or overly repetitive.
1	Limited or inappropriate organisation of musical ideas.

What are the rules for completing the task?

The composition must be completed under controlled conditions.

Preparation time will include the following:

- Learning and practising composition techniques
- Learning how to use any technology required for the task
- Experimentation with the available sound sources and technology
- Finding samples as appropriate to the brief
- Developing draft melodic, harmonic and rhythmic ideas for later input into the live file (the work-in-progress)
- Annotating draft scores with new ideas and comments.

Any of the above may be undertaken in school/college or at home – it does not need to be directly supervised, but your teacher will need to regularly monitor your progress as you develop your composition ideas.

When you do any work to the file that will eventually be mixed down into a stereo track for submission to the examiner (the work-in-progress) it is considered 'writing time', so you must observe the following rules:

1. All composition work must be your own, including any tracks that are to be performed by other people. The only exception is when you have used samples or loops that are acceptable as clearly stated in the brief, in which case you must declare their use in the logbook.
2. You must complete all the input, importing, recording, editing, processing and mixing of the composition under supervision by your teacher or another member of staff.
3. The live file (the work-in-progress) must stay on the school/college premises at all times (you can't take it home or access it from home), but you may print out a score and take this home for annotation or burn it to a finalised audio CD (check with your teacher before taking any work out of controlled conditions).
4. Any preparation work you bring into school/college must be checked by your teacher/supervisor before you restart 'writing time'.
5. You can access the internet during your preparation time, but not during inputting, importing, recording, editing, processing and mixing of your composition.
6. You must complete the input, importing, recording, editing, processing and mixing of the composition within 20 hours (this does not include any preparation time).

Completing the composition

As with the arranging task, it is important to take stock of what material is available before launching into the creative process of coming up with your own musical ideas. This is not a free composition – it must follow a set brief.

Fulfilling the brief

Read through the three set briefs. You will probably have a preferred method of working by now and know which area you feel most comfortable in, but do read through all three briefs in case something grabs your imagination in a way you weren't expecting. You will always be required to write for at least six separate tracks or instrumental parts, although the individual briefs may be more precise about the exact forces required. Each brief will require a different approach from the outset.

Brief 1: Music for film or television

Tellingly, this brief starts with a mention of how important it is to use music technology in your composition. This will be mentioned again in more detail, but you should note that, like the arranging mark scheme, there are 10 marks allocated for the use of music tech. In the composition however, the emphasis is more on how you have used sound shaping and effects to develop musical ideas rather than how well you have sequenced the parts. Therefore it is insufficient to produce a great orchestral score with no music tech input – in order to gain full marks you must consider music tech as another musical element that needs developing, just like melody and harmony.

After the introduction laying the ground rules, you are presented with a scene you have to write music to. How precise or descriptive this is will differ from year to year, but the principle will always be the same – you have to write some music to accompany onscreen action, either to serve as a backdrop or to set the mood/heighten tension and reinforce the visual elements of the plot. Try to capture the scene in your imagination.

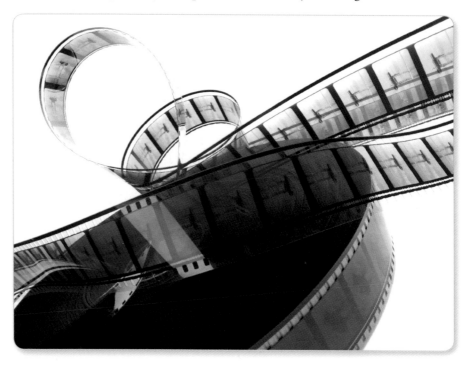

You will then be given some practical instructions as to how you should write the music – for example, you may be asked to create a set of samples or you may be given some restrictions in instrumentation. Play through the scene in your head, imagining how these sound sources would work along with the visuals. What would you hear if you were at the cinema and a similar scene was happening onscreen? How could the sound sources be used creatively to achieve this effect?

You will then be given a quite precise plan, describing approximately three minutes of action, separating the time into distinct scenes that will require different approaches as to how you use the musical resources to capture the appropriate mood. You should draw up a storyboard of some sort, listing your ideas and **paying close attention to the timings**. If you ignore the timings, you will not score many marks for the first criterion, responding to the set brief. Stick as closely as possible to the given timings, trying to keep each section to exactly the length of time given in the brief. Also pay attention to the demands of the brief regarding linking the sections – does it require a short gap between sections or do you have to make the sections flow into each other?

Brief 2: Electro-acoustic music

This brief will probably be less precise in its exact demands, leaving you more room for your imagination to run riot, however, to be successful in this brief you must stick rigidly to the instructions on what sound sources you can use and the overall effect requested. You will have free rein to develop the sound sources as you see fit, so one of the first things you should do, after gathering the necessary samples, is to experiment with the sound-shaping tools at your disposal, stretching, squashing, shifting and otherwise twisting the original samples out of all recognition and generally having a great deal of fun. Don't worry, enjoying your work is permitted by the specification!

The key points with this brief are to significantly manipulate the permitted sound sources, using music technology as your main developmental tool and to ensure that the whole piece is coherent, with a clear sense of direction and structure, unifying the elements in some way. One approach is to think of a way you might make the sampled material imitate the function of standard instruments – for example, you might make some short, percussive sounds to fulfil a rhythmic function, some long, sustaining sounds that contain pitch elements to act as a chordal pad and some more abrasive or distinctive timbres to act as the lead instruments. Ensure you cover the full frequency spectrum to keep things sonically interesting. It is a very good idea to listen to a variety of works by electro-acoustic composers (such as Varèse, Stockhausen, Xenakis, and Eno) before undertaking this task to get an idea of how they organise their music.

Brief 3: A popular song

This brief should start with a few health warnings:

○ Do not try to make a song you have previously written fit into the given brief
○ You must complete the entire composition by yourself – you are not permitted to submit any element of group work
○ A popular song should contain the same rigorous approach to the use of music technology and development of ideas as a composition that follows the other two briefs – it is not an easy option.

This brief is sometimes a harder option with regards to development of musical ideas, because it does not naturally lend itself to musical development in the same way as brief 2 for example, where development is fundamental to the whole task. You may find song-writing quite easy, in which case this may be the brief for you to attempt, but you should still take a step back and ensure that you are meeting all the requirements of the mark scheme.

The use of music technology in your song is another area that needs care and attention. It is not enough simply to record a set of standard rock band instruments, because this will not really meet the requirements of criterion 3: manipulation of sounds. A straightforward way to fulfil this criterion would be to investigate the use of some original guitar effects or interesting, home-brewed synth sounds, making these a central element in your song.

Achieving a coherent sense of style

All compositions need to have a consistent sense of style and a clear sense of direction. You should strive to ensure that your composition has some element that underpins the whole piece, for example a particular sound-world, a reoccurring melodic/rhythmic motif or a chord structure. It is important that each section of your composition feels like it belongs somehow to the others, that the beginning and ending of the piece feel satisfying, and the middle sections flow naturally from one to the other. Development of your ideas also falls into this category – if you can use a few important musical ideas in different ways in the different sections, there will automatically be sense of unity across the sections.

Brief 1: Music for film or television often poses the most problems in terms of achieving a sense of coherence due to the nature of having several short sections creating distinct moods or reflecting widely varying onscreen activities. As such, it is most important in this brief to think of unifying elements across the different sections – perhaps using a melodic idea in different ways, or bringing a rhythmic feature to the fore. Listen to how some film composers have used the 'hero's motif' in different ways to reflect the situations the hero has found himself in. The use of the motif instantly identifies what the film is, and the setting of the motif (for example victorious music, a sense of melancholy and so on) will immediately paint a picture of what the mood is at the time. Having said this, ensure that you do not make each section sound so similar that they don't have enough individuality to reflect the specific elements required by the brief.

Brief 2: Electro-acoustic music poses its own set of problems in that it is difficult to sustain a piece of music that does not have a traditional key, chord sequence and/or melody for any length of time while maintaining both a sense of direction and enough interest across the whole duration of the piece. It is important to determine a structure and some draft timings from the outset, treating development of the samples and sounds as a structural tool. Varying the texture is paramount to the success of a piece based on timbre rather than harmony. Listen to some of the atonal music of Schoenberg to hear how he keeps the listener's interest throughout – the use of exciting dynamics, wide pitch ranges and sudden textural contrasts play an important role. Think of ways to achieve these goals using the elements at your disposal. Remember that you can manipulate the samples as you see fit, so if you are lacking a low frequency sound, get busy with the pitch shift and low shelving EQ!

It is perfectly feasible for a brief 2 piece to contain traditional harmonies/chord sequences and melodies, but even if it is a traditionally structured, tonal composition, the features mentioned above should still be considered of paramount importance.

It is much easier to achieve a sense of coherence in brief 3: popular song. In order to be successful in this criterion, the song should have a coherent sense of style (not necessarily a recognisable pop music style) and show some development of the musical ideas. Development is the area that will require most attention for this brief.

Using music technology

It is fundamental to this task to make imaginative use of music technology. It is not enough to write a good piece for traditional instruments – it must make use of some aspect(s) of technology as an integral part of the piece, not just as a method of recording or notating ideas.

The section in the mark scheme rewarding the use of music technology is split into two sections – criterion 3: manipulation of sounds and criterion 4: quality of recorded submission. We will deal with criterion 4 first, because it is something that has been discussed previously (for task 1A). The quality of the final stereo audio track is important, particularly because this is a music technology GCE so any submitted work should be of the highest possible audio quality, no matter what aspects of that work are being examined.

There are several aspects to consider in order to achieve the highest marks for this category:

- The lead in should be no more than two seconds
- Notes should not be cut off at the start or end of the audio track
- Distortion or clipping must be avoided while maintaining a high overall recording level
- There should be no clicks, hiss, noise or other artefacts introduced to the audio when mixing to stereo
- Any reverb tail at the end of the composition should decay naturally
- Any fade out should be smooth
- Any silence at the end of the fadeout/reverb tail should not exceed two seconds.

Manipulation of sounds using music technology

The amount of sound-mangling technology available nowadays is quite bewildering. As computer-based recording has become more entrenched, the computer's processing power has been harnessed to do all sorts of interesting things to the digital audio. You must experiment with the tools you have at your disposal – this will depend on the sequencing package you use and the effects units available to you, but you will have a veritable sonic arsenal at your disposal, even if your school/college has limited resources. The early music technology pioneers such as Stockhausen sometimes took years to complete their compositions because they had a sound in their heads that they wanted to realise, but the technology did not exist in order to produce this sound, so they had to either develop existing technology or invent new pieces of equipment. Try to tap into this pioneering spirit when you are composing.

Try the following:

1. Investigate the extreme settings of any effects units and processing tools you have available – don't go with the presets or 'recommended' settings – turn everything up to 11!

2. Investigate what happens when you gradually alter one parameter while the others are at their minimum or maximum settings

3. Connect pieces of equipment in unusual configurations

4. Detune audio as far as you can, then detune the resultant audio as far as you can again

5. Time stretch to the maximum/minimum settings, then time stretch the resultant audio again

6. Apply extreme filters and EQ settings to normal sounds

7. Try reversing all the resultant audio from the above experiments

8. Juxtapose contrasting timbres (e.g. a percussive sound and a sustaining sound) applying processing as if they were one single timbre

9. Juxtapose different treatments of the same timbre

10. Check out all the extreme settings on your guitar pedals and connect them in different ways

11. Feed the output of a device back into its input (be careful with this one)

12. Set up new synth timbres using extreme pitch settings and 'wrong' combinations/effects settings

13. Play the mixing desk as if it was an instrument

14. Set up different mics with gain levels at the point so that they will just start to feedback, setup different EQs on each channel, and experiment with moving the faders up and down to get different feedback pitches

15. Apply rhythmic delays and extreme reverb settings to all the above

16. Take the most interesting audio artefacts produced by the above experiments and use these, disregarding the other stuff

17. This is the area that really makes this subject interesting, so let your imagination run riot!

After all the experimentation you need to narrow down the possible options into sounds that will work in the context of your composition. A good way to do this is to limit yourself in some way – for example, you might decide to see what sounds you can get from one piece of kit rather than using all the equipment available, so as to keep the sound-world coherent.

Try to use music technology as a developmental tool in the same way as you would develop a traditional melody or harmony – you might state an idea and then develop it in gradually more obscure ways, leading the listener through your composition as opposed to pushing them off the cliff of sudden sonic annihilation.

Remember to keep to the brief at all times.

Developing ideas

All compositions must develop musical ideas using technology – this is one of the compulsory criteria, but the other ways in which you will develop your ideas will depend largely on what brief you have chosen, so you should consider the optional criteria appropriate to the style of your composition. For example, it is unlikely that an electro-acoustic soundscape will score too many marks in the melody criterion (although this is not a hard and fast rule), so you will probably want to consider the texture criterion as one of the options. It is extremely important to ensure that your composition can be assessed in three of the optional criteria – if there is little melodic or harmonic detail for an examiner to assess, make sure that there is enough in the rhythm, texture and form/structure areas for your composition to score marks.

The next section offers some ways to help get you started in developing your musical ideas. It is not comprehensive, so do not feel you have to restrict yourself to the concepts covered here – if you come up with different, imaginative ways of developing your ideas, then so much the better!

- Melody
- Rhythm
- Texture
- Form/structure.

Melody

Some people have the knack of instantly creating memorable melodies that work with any given chord sequence or context. If this is you, then you probably won't need to read this section, but if this isn't you, don't worry, because you are not alone. It is possible to take a more workmanlike approach to the creation and development of melodies and still end up with what a listener will regard as a strong, imaginative melody.

Melody contains several musical ingredients – pitch, tonality, harmony and rhythm – and because it has to be delivered by a voice or instrument of some sort, it will depend to some extent on the timbre of the voice/ instrument singing/playing it. There may also be an element of noise introduced into a melody to make it more interesting – if you listen to chart songs, the lead vocal part often contains quite a lot of effects to try and capture the individual character of the singer (such as vocal scoops, sighs, cracking or breaking of the voice and so on). As such, melody can be quite an intuitive thing, so if you come up with something you feel happy with by pure inspiration, record it in some way and roll with it.

Take a simple three-note idea, for example C, G, A.

What can you do with this motif?

1. Give it different rhythms:

2. Play the notes in different octaves:

3.   Turn the motif upside down (invert it):

4.   Play it backwards (retrograde):

5.   Play it upside down and backwards (retrograde inversion):

6.   Play it in sequence, ascending:

or descending:

The sequence does not have to be one tone – it could be anything.

7.   Break it into its component intervals and develop these in sequence:

This could be taken in all sorts of directions with almost endless possibilities.

8.   Stretch or compress the wider intervals:

9.   Change key from major to minor or vice versa:

10. Introduce passing notes and ornamentation:

Of course, these can be used in any combination or not at all, but it should give you an idea of how you can develop your melodic ideas. It generally works best if you develop one aspect at a time rather than applying several simultaneous methods of development, rendering your melody unrecognisable from the original motif, or if you move away from the original by gradually increasing the amount of complexity. It is also important to consider how the melody works with the harmony at all times – whether you want a harmonious, concordant feel or deliberately want to create tension by using notes that clash with the harmony of the moment. Remember that you can repeat notes in your melodic motif – it is not necessary for the pitch to change on every note.

One of the best examples of exploration of a simple melodic motif can be heard in the first movement of Beethoven's fifth symphony, where he took a simple, four-note motif and developed it into an entire symphonic movement, using it both melodically and in all the accompaniment parts.

Rhythm

Rhythmic ideas can often be just as important as melodic ideas in creating a memorable hook or motif. For example, in the Beethoven symphony, the rhythm is integral to the melodic motif. This example shows that it is sometimes very difficult to separate the rhythmic content from the pitch content of a melody (doing so is an interesting developmental technique in itself). As such, rhythmic development often occurs in the context of melodic development too.

For unpitched percussion, there is no melodic content, so rhythms have to be developed on their own. In this case it is often with regard to where the rhythm falls in the bar or in relation to the strong beats of the bar. Rhythmic displacement is a common form of rhythmic development – taking an idea and shifting the accents off the strong beats and onto the start of the short rhythmic motif, regardless of where it falls in the bar.

Other examples of rhythmic development include:

1. Adding anticipation/syncopation to an originally straight, on-beat rhythm
2. Adding cross rhythms and additional rhythms to an existing rhythmic idea
3. Leaving notes out of a beat or adding notes
4. Augmentation – increasing the durations of some/all of the notes
5. Diminution – decreasing the durations of some/all of the notes
6. Forcing a rhythm into a new time signature (e.g. taking the 'Mission Impossible' $\frac{5}{4}$ rhythm and forcing it into $\frac{4}{4}$).

As for melody, it is best not to use too many of these ideas simultaneously. In fact, it takes only fairly minor changes to rhythmic motives before the original idea becomes unrecognisable on just listening (as opposed to studying a notated score).

Texture

All pieces will require textural contrast in order to maintain interest across the duration of the piece. Refer to the section on texture for task 1C (page 65) for some general ideas. In addition to these general points, you should ensure that your texture helps to fulfil the brief, paying particular attention to this area if you have chosen brief 1: music for film or television.

Instrumentation is specifically referred to in criterion 3: manipulation of sounds in the specification, but in addition to the work you do on the manipulation of timbres, your choices of instrumentation, timbres and combinations of these will have significant influence on the texture of your composition, so they may gain additional credit in this criterion.

If you have chosen brief 2: electro-acoustic music, you should take special care to ensure that you have made full use of textural contrasts throughout your composition (as appropriate) to ensure that you can score the full range of marks in this criterion.

Form/structure

Refer to the section on structure for task 1C (page 64) for general information.

Structure in your composition will depend largely on your choice of brief – If you choose brief 1: music for film and television, the large-scale structure has been chosen for you, it is just left to you to decide how to structure the ideas within the overall framework. For brief 2: electro-acoustic music, the structure is likely to be something completely new and original that you have come up with to meet the requirements of the sounds you have developed. It may not be a traditional structure in the sense of section A–B–A–C and so on, but may have more to do with the interplay between textures and how you build them up. If you choose brief 3: a popular song, you may follow a typical song structure as the bare-bones of your composition, but you will need to do something more imaginative with it. For example making interesting use of links between sections, use of tonality as a structural device (perhaps including unusual, but successful key changes from section to section) or finding an unpredictable, but satisfying new way of using the main sections commonly used in a popular song.

Finalising your composition

As with all the tasks, leave enough time so that you can step back from your work for a while after the completion of your first draft and return to it, at least two or three days later with fresh ears. Always apply the mark scheme to your work, asking yourself if you can hear everything that is necessary to gain full marks in each criterion. If you can't hear the work you have put into developing ideas and timbres simply by listening to the final audio track, you should consider writing a commentary to go along with your work outlining the pertinent points and insert it into the logbook after questions 8 and 9.

Completing the logbook

The two questions in the logbook referring to task 3C simply ask for details of the equipment and any samples you used. This does not give the examiner much to go on when assessing how you have come up with and developed your musical ideas. The only specification requirements are that you submit the final audio track and the logbook. You may wish to consider whether it is appropriate to hand in additional materials in order to support your submission, especially if you have used compositional techniques that, although clearly creditworthy according to the mark scheme, are not at all obvious in the audio alone. A score is not required, but you may decide it best to submit an annotated score or a thorough description of the composition, highlighting any points of interest. Any additional paperwork is entirely optional – your work will still be assessed even if you have just submitted the audio tracks and the logbook.

What can I expect in the exam?

There will be 5 questions in the exam, split into two sections for a total of 80 marks. Section A will contain 4 questions and will carry 62 marks. Section B will consist of question 5 only and will carry 18 marks. Area of study 1: the principles and practice of music technology and area of study 3: the development of technology-based music will be examined in this unit. Overall, unit 4 is worth 40% of the A2 or 20% of the full GCE. The examination will be taken in June of the A2 year and it will last for 2 hours.

The following table summarises the contents of the examination paper for unit 4:

	Section A		Section B	Unit 4 Summary
Question Number	1–3	4	5	5 questions
Area of Study	1 and 3	3	1	AoS 1 and 3
Marks	46	16	18	80 Marks
% of A2	23%	8%	9%	40% of A2

The examination paper is mostly a practical task completed under examination conditions. You will receive a question paper, an audio CD containing a series of music files that you will have to import onto a computer audio sequencing package (such as Cubase or Logic) and a blank CD. Any computer package used will need to have the ability to import and manipulate audio files, including all the basic functions you would need if you were mixing down a multi-track recording. Read on through the chapter to see exactly what the examination demands to ensure that your software is up to the task.

What will the questions ask?

You will be asked to respond to a series of questions that will give clear instructions as to what you need to do with the audio material provided on the CD. This will include importing the samples, editing them in some way, using them to create a complete track and mixing them down to a final stereo track to be exported onto the blank CD. There will always be 5 questions (most of which will be subdivided into several, smaller questions) and they will be arranged as follows:

○ Questions 1–3
○ Question 4
○ Question 5.

Questions 1–3

On the audio CD there will be a selection of tracks including the following:

1. A melody part
2. A harmony/chordal part (such as a guitar or keyboard part)

3. A bass line
4. A drum and/or percussion part.

The tracks may be complete or they may come in small sections that you have to compile into a complete track. Several of the tracks will have errors of some kind that you need to correct before you get to the final mixdown stage. Anything you have to do with the provided audio tracks will be clearly stated in the exam paper. Possible processes include:

- Trimming
- Normalising
- Dynamics processing
- Adding effects
- EQing
- Panning
- Compiling a complete track from segments
- Adjusting tempo.

An example of this would be to import several short drum samples, trim them to an appropriate length, change the dynamics and/or tempo of one or more of the samples so that they all match precisely and then link them together to form a complete drum track.

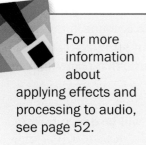

For more information about applying effects and processing to audio, see page 52.

The specification states that a MIDI keyboard should be available (attached to the computer workstation). It is possible that you will be required to input and edit some MIDI data in addition to importing and manipulating the audio tracks. Some typical tasks you will be required to do may include inputting an additional percussion part to supplement the drums or an extra keyboard pad sound doubling the chord part.

Questions 1–3 will also test your knowledge of musical elements and notation. There will always be an element of staff notation in the exam paper that you have to compare with the audio you have imported. The staff notation will have some errors in pitch or rhythm that you must identify from listening to the audio. It is acceptable to make use of the MIDI keyboard to assist you in this task. There may be some questions asking you to identify similarities or differences between the tracks on the audio CD provided, or to discuss some production techniques that have been applied to the audio (or should have been applied, but haven't).

There will also be at least one general question on some aspect of using music technology in a practical way, linked in some way, but not necessarily directly referring to the audio on the CD provided. For example there may be a question on some general sequencing or recording techniques that may have been used to generate/capture one of the tracks on the CD. For this question, knowledge of area of study 3: the development of technology-based music may be required in addition to an understanding of the practices and principles of music technology (area of study 1).

For any questions requiring processing of the audio in any way, you will be required to submit a WAV file of your response much in the same way as you would write your answer on a traditional question paper. For example, if you were required to apply some dynamics processing to a track, you would have to save the processed track as a wav file for marking by the examiner. This is seen as a much more effective way of examining how well you understand music technology – it is one thing to write about it, but quite another to do it successfully! This highlights the importance of ensuring you know how to use all the basic processing tools on your audio sequencing package. The best way to gain an understanding of these tools is by using them practically, so when you are completing your practical work for unit 3, ensure you understand what you are doing rather than just tweaking a few controls in the hope that a better sound will magically come out the other end. If you do not fully understand any of the parameters of the plugins and effects units you are working with, make sure you ask your teacher to explain (and preferably demonstrate) what they do. Some parameters have very little audible effect on certain sounds, but it is good to understand why they have been included (perhaps as some error-correction facility). You will be working under severe time restrictions when you are taking the examination paper for unit 4, so there will not be time to figure out the equipment from scratch. Try to make sure that the basic operation of all the equipment you will use in the examination has become second nature while you have been completing your work for unit 3.

Question 4

This question requires an extended, written response. It will always be worth 16 marks and is the one place in the exam where the quality of your written communication (QWC) is taken into account in the marks awarded for your response. The question will be on some aspect of area of study 3: the development of technology-based music that relates in some way to the audio on the CD provided.

The following is a list of the topics that questions will be drawn from:

Development of:

- Synthesisers
- Electric guitars and amplification
- Samplers and drum machines
- Use of effects units and processors across time
- Development of recording media including multi-track recording.

Digital recording including an awareness of:

- Computer-based recording (including knowledge of typical software packages)
- Hard disk/standalone recorders
- Computer-hosted virtual instruments/effects
- The impact of MIDI on recording and performing
- Use of the internet as a resource and for communication between artists
- The context of all the above and the impact of technology on producers, engineers and artists.

There will always be a choice of two questions from the topics listed above – you must answer one of these two questions.

The following is a paraphrased mark scheme. The specific detail relating directly to the question will change from year to year, but the general descriptions of each level will not differ by much. As such, only the general descriptions have been included here. Each year, an additional list of all the appropriate points relating to the question will be used by examiners to check that you have included direct answers to the question rather than just constructing a nice, wordy essay with little actual content. Pay particular attention to references to the quality of written communication (QWC). It is not necessary to achieve every aspect of a given level to score a mark in that level – a best-fit approach is used for this mark scheme. For example, it is possible to score in the 2–5 level for QWC, but still achieve a mark of 9 out of 16 because the actual content was very good, if poorly presented. It is not necessary to complete your answer in continuous prose – bullet points are acceptable if they are a more efficient way to organise your response, but your answer must still be structured appropriately.

Mark	
14 – 16	An excellent and perceptive response. Every aspect of the question has been thoroughly dealt with in the answer. The response has been well structured so that there is a clear sense of the order of events as appropriate to the subject. QWC: There are very few spelling problems and all language is used correctly. The answer is well organised throughout.
10 – 13	A good response. Most aspects of the question have been dealt with in the answer. The response has been structured so that there is a sense of the order of events as appropriate to the subject. QWC: There are a few spelling problems but most language is used correctly. The answer is well organised.
6 – 9	An acceptable response. Some reference has been made to the main topic of the question, with some justification for any answers given, but there is not a lot of detail. The response has been structured to some extent, but there is little sense of the order in which things occurred. QWC: There are some problems with spelling and the choice of language – some words may be used incorrectly. The answer is mostly coherent.
2 – 5	A limited response. Some references have been made to the topic of the question, but there are no reasons given for the answers and there is little detail. The response has not been structured well and does not place events in a timeline. QWC: There are quite a few problems with spelling and the choice of language – some words are used incorrectly. The answer is organised in places.
1	A poor response with little reference to any relevant points. QWC: There are frequent problems with spelling and the choice of language – many words may be used incorrectly. The answer is poorly organised.

Since the question is worth 16 marks, include 16 different points all related to the question itself, supporting any opinions with factual evidence and justifying any answers you give. It is important to have a plan before attempting to write your response. Read the question several times, making sure you really understand what is being asked. There is no point writing everything you know about some random aspect of music technology, because you can only get credit for points relating directly to the question itself, and if you go off on a tangent, merrily waffling on, you are likely to lose marks for the coherence of your response.

On a scrap piece of paper, or in the space provided on the exam paper for planning your response, note any of the relevant facts that you can remember that directly answer the question – any points will need to be backed up with a reason or justification for their inclusion, so make sure you can explain everything clearly.

Organise your ideas in date order – the points may have come to you in a fairly random order as they sprang to mind, so now number them in chronological order. To score in the top bracket you need to give the examiner a sense that you know how one development led to another.

Include appropriate musical and music tech vocabulary, but don't try to over-complicate your response with big words in case you use them incorrectly.

Having planned your response, put it into prose or bullet points, making sure you address each point in order. Avoid repetition and padding – there is nothing more likely to antagonise an examiner.

Read through your response to ensure that it makes sense. Do not assume any knowledge on the part of the examiner – make sure all the detail is in your response. The more detail the better – as long as it directly answers the question!

Question 5 – Section B

Section B is worth 18 marks out of the total of 80 for the whole paper. It consists of one question – question 5.

'Produce a final balanced stereo mix using appropriate effects and transfer the final mix to your CD.' It is possible that the question will be as simple as this, with a mark scheme similar to a simplified version of that used for tasks 1B and 3B, but it is also possible that you will be asked to do specific things in the mix, such as putting a particular type of reverb onto the vocal part, a different reverb onto the guitar, adding delay to one of the tracks, adding a filter to one part and so on, in which case the mark scheme will be a little more complex, addressing each of the areas in a little more detail. Question 5 will always ask you to produce a stereo mix of all the tracks you have imported and edited. **Note that if you do not produce a final mix, you will not score any of the available 18 marks. Leave enough time for your mixdown!** Save the final mix as a wav file.

Refer to the section on mixing and adding effects in task 1B (pages 52–54) for more details of how to achieve best results.

The final mix will be assessed on three categories:

1. Blend and balance
2. Use of stereo field
3. Use of effects.

These categories will not necessarily be worth 6 marks each – the way in which they will be subdivided depends on the audio material you are provided with.

The following is an example of how the marks may be allocated:

Blend and Balance	6	All the tracks are mixed well, giving an excellent overall sound. Everything is balanced with all the parts audible and at an appropriate level. If parts are meant to blend in together, they do so and if they are meant to stand out, they do so.
	4 – 5	Most of the tracks have been well balanced. There may be a few moments where something is not as loud or soft as it needs to be or there are a few areas where parts do not blend as well as they could, but the mix is generally successful.
	2 – 3	The mix works from time to time, but often there are areas where parts do not blend in together or there are times when important parts are lost in the mix. Some tracks may be far too quiet or far too loud.
	1	The mix really takes away from the success of the recording. There are many areas where parts are lost or drown everything else out. Tracks do not blend well.
Use of Stereo Field	6	The track has a real sense of width with all the tracks panned appropriately. The panning adds to the sense of space without leaving any big gaps in the middle.
	4 – 5	Good use has been made of the stereo field with few misjudgements in where the parts have been placed. The sense of stereo may not be as wide as it could be or there may be a bit of a 'hole in the middle'.
	2 – 3	There are some errors in where tracks have been placed in the stereo field (e.g. strong parts are misplaced or unbalanced resulting in a sense of one side being more dominant than the other). The stereo field may feel restricted.
	1	Very little (or no) use has been made of the stereo field or there are some very serious errors in where instruments have been placed.
Use of Effects	6	Effects have been used carefully and effectively to enhance the recording. All the effects used have been well chosen.
	4 – 5	The effects used have been mostly well chosen. There may be the odd instance where a track is slightly too dry or wet, but it does not take away from the recording.
	2 – 3	Effects have been used in the track, but there may be some poor choices or two or more tracks are too dry or wet, noticeably detracting from the quality of the recording.
	1	Many of the tracks are far too dry or wet, significantly detracting from the quality of the recording. Several effects may have been poorly chosen.

What do I need to know?

○ Area of study 1: the principles and practice of music technology
○ Area of study 3: the development of music technology.

Area of study 1: the principles and practice of music technology

You need to have a firm understanding of the way your audio sequencing package works and have a command of its plug-in effects. It is especially important to know how to successfully apply compression and reverb within the audio sequencing package.

Questions may arise on any of the practical elements of sequencing and multi-track recording you have completed so far. These questions will be related to the audio material provided by Edexcel, but it is possible that one or more of the tracks on the CD originated as a MIDI sequence before being converted to audio, so there are just as likely to be questions arising on sequencing skills as there are on recording skills. Revise all the material covered in unit 1 regarding sequencing skills and recording techniques for different instruments. Make reference to techniques you have discovered for yourself in your responses – this is a practical subject, so much of the learning is done on the job.

Area of Study 3: The Development of Technology Based Music

Over the last century, developments in music technology have largely been driven by the demands of composers and the music industry. For example, the electronic music composers of the mid-20th century needed more advanced synthesis capabilities than were available to them at the time, so they needed to develop new equipment in order to realise the sounds in their heads. Similarly, recording technology has imposed limitations on what artists can achieve in the recording studio, so they have pushed the development of recording technology in order to realise their creative ambitions. As such, this area of study goes alongside area of study 2: popular music styles since 1910, but focuses on the technology itself rather than the music or stylistic fingerprints. You will therefore already have studied a lot of what you need to know for this element of the course when you were looked at the development of popular music across the last 100 years.

Question 4 in the examination paper for unit 4 will present a choice of two questions on the development of music technology as it relates to some feature of the audio material on the examination CD. The two options will always present two very different angles on the development of music technology, so it is likely that there is one option that will leap out as being the one for you, while you may feel less comfortable with the other – do not worry if this is the case, just go for the option that sits best in your field of expertise.

It is beyond the scope of this book to present an in-depth study of the development of music technology across the last 100 years, but the following is a summary of what you should learn:

Development of synthesisers, electric guitars and amplification (i.e. the development of instruments that plug in and ways of amplifying them) and the development of samplers and drum machines.

- The first examples of use of the technology: e.g., the first use of a pickup on a guitar
- The reasons for the development of the technology: e.g., the guitarist wanted to be heard in a big band context
- The development of the technology related to changes in the pop music industry: e.g., amplification gets bigger with more distortion available to meet the demands of guitarists in the 1960s

- Any major innovations that changed the way people view/play the instruments: e.g., development of digital synthesis
- Pros and cons of the developments: e.g., there has been a revival of analogue synthesis because many people like the sound it makes and have grown to love the imperfections, so they will put up with the inherent problems that digital synthesis was created to solve
- Use of effects units and processors across time
- The development from large, physical units such as reverb plates and spring reverbs to compact digital devices
- The historical reason for the original use of effects and processors: e.g., equalisation developed as a means of combating inherent problems with the recording technology (rather than as a creative tool)
- Development of recording media
- A general knowledge of the recording media used across the last 100 years
- The media used for mass distribution of recorded material (e.g., vinyl, cassette tape, CD, MP3).

Advent of multi-track recording

- Digital recording
- The development of computer based recording, including the development of input/output devices such as multi-channel sound cards and external firewire/USB devices
- The development of software packages to facilitate the use of the computer hardware: e.g., how the MIDI-only packages such as Notator developed into powerful audio editing packages such as Logic and the parallel development of computer processing power and sophistication
- Virtual instruments and effects: how increased processing power was harnessed to put different instruments and effects units in one box (the computer), instead of having many hardware equivalents, and the impact this has had on home recording and the recording industry in general.

MIDI

- The development of the MIDI 1.0 specification in the 1980s
- The impact of this new connectivity standard on the development of synthesisers
- The impact of MIDI on performing: use of MIDI backings, connecting keyboards and effects units, development of MIDI guitar and drums etc.
- Impact of MIDI on recording: sequenced parts used alongside live recordings, synchronising MIDI to audio and so on.

The internet

- How it is used as a resource for samples, MIDI files, listening to music etc.
- How it can be used for artists in different locations to communicate with each other, including the ability to record albums even when the various performers are in different countries

Note that study for the use of the internet does not include its use as a tool for marketing and distribution of music (e.g., iTunes and other download sites, YouTube and so on).

All of the above focus on the developments of the technology and the impact this has had on the artists, producers and engineers, but they do not focus on the music industry itself – you will not be examined on the workings of record companies, marketing, distribution etc.

For all the above you should have a good idea of the order in which things occurred/were developed and some idea of key dates (for example, MIDI 1.0 spec released in 1983). Marks will be available for knowing key dates, but they will not be the main focus of the question – it is much more important to have an understanding of the context and impact of major developments rather than just be able to recite facts. See pages 127–131 of the specification for a list of recommended further reading resources.

Exam technique and practical issues

- Preparing equipment
- Exam technique
- Preparing final submission material.

Preparing equipment

The final, two hour examination for unit 4 must be completed under exam conditions. It is therefore essential to ensure that all the equipment you are going to use functions exactly as you expect it to. Check that the audio sequencing package is correctly set up, that it is enabled for importing audio and that all the necessary effects plug-ins are functioning normally. Check the orientation of headphones (left is left and right is right) and that both sides produce an even volume and frequency response – listen to some material you are very familiar with as test material. It would be a good idea to have a dry run on your equipment using past exam papers or the sample assessment materials shortly before the exam itself.

By confirming that all the equipment is fully functional and free from any gremlins, you will find it easier to relax into the exam itself.

There is time allowed at the beginning of the examination to check that all the equipment is functioning properly (before the actual 2 hours exam time begins), but you should be confident that everything functions properly before exam conditions commence. Ensure you are ready for this exam earlier than would be expected for other exams due to the nature of the technical equipment used.

Exam technique

To achieve the best possible results in any exam, it is not enough just to know all the answers: you must know how to communicate them to the examiner and how to approach the paper itself. How you approach the exam will depend on your own strengths and weaknesses, time management skills, writing skills, command of the equipment and so on, but there are several general tips you might find useful:

1. Set yourself a strict time budget for each question based on (a) the mark allocation for each section (b) your experience of how long you need per question based on practise papers.

2. Do not exceed your time allocation by being overly perfectionist about tiny details in questions 1–3: remember that there are lots of marks to strive for in the other parts of the paper that will need this time. The law of diminishing returns states that, after a while, it takes a lot of effort to produce a small improvement, so make sure the basics are in place before trying to make tiny improvements.

3. Attempt the questions in the order 1–2–3–5–4. This way you will ensure you get the mix completed (if you don't do a final mix you would lose 18 marks, but you will always be able to write something, even just a few sentences if struggling for time on question 4). Also, you will have mix ideas from when you were working with the individual tracks and don't want to break your train of thought with the extended writing question.

4. If there are any questions you particularly struggle with, weigh up how important they are in the grand scheme of things and approach them accordingly. For example, if you struggle to find the errors in pitch, check how much this is worth. If it is only 3 or 4 marks, leave it and come back to it if you have time rather than going over your time allocation for something that may not gain you marks anyway.

5. Always plan question 4 before starting to write, even if you are short on time. If you don't have long left, get some basic thoughts down and order them appropriately, don't just launch into writing anything that comes into your head. A minute spent planning will reap many times that reward in the coherence of your response, even if you get fewer words written as a result of the minute less.

Preparing final submission material

When you are seated at your computer workstation, immediately before the exam begins, but under exam conditions, you should open your audio sequencing package, create a new project and set the tempo as instructed in the exam paper. Import track 1 from the audio CD and check that it plays back properly on your system. Check that the bars align correctly. You should then stop and wait until instructed to begin your examination. On this instruction your two hours begin.

Attempt the exam using the exam techniques given above, preparing final WAV files for any audio to be submitted to the examiner as instructed in the exam paper. The exam paper will give further instructions as to what you should do with the completed WAV files after the exam ends. It is likely that you will have to burn this onto CD, but there may be options in future years to upload the WAV files to a secure server. Read the instructions on the exam paper carefully, because the audio is just as important as the physical paper you have completed – if the examiner does not have access to the audio they cannot award you any marks. Any burning of audio CDs or uploading of WAV files to a secure server will take place after the two hours of the exam time have been completed.

Well done – you have now completed your course!

It is hoped that the skills you have developed and the knowledge you have acquired in following the GCE Music Technology course will equip you in whatever direction you wish to take your studies of music technology from here. Remember – always be your own harshest critic, whatever path your career may take, and enjoy the journey.

Balance: The volume of instruments or parts relative to each other.

Clipping: Exceeding the maximum volume specification of a given device. Digital clipping produces a particularly unpleasant sound, but clipping in an analogue device is sometimes acceptable.

Cutoff frequency: The nominal value at which a filter has an audible effect on the frequency range of a sound. Normally applied to Low Pass Filters in which case the cutoff frequency describes the highest audible frequency.

Chorus: A form of modulation combining a slightly delayed and detuned version of a sound with the original to produce a thickening effect.

Compression: A method of 'squeezing' the dynamic range of a signal by reducing the signal level above a user-defined threshold by a user-defined ratio. The resultant signal is normally boosted so that the whole signal is perceived to be louder than before compression had been applied.

Cross-rhythm: Different rhythmic patterns performed simultaneously.

Delay: A time domain effect in which the original signal is repeated one or more times. There is normally a decrease in volume and high frequency content with each repeat.

Dry/wet: A dry signal is an original, unprocessed signal; a wet signal has been effected in some way.

EQ: Equalisation – originally a method of compensating for deficiencies in the frequency response of recording and playback equipment, EQ is now used as a way of cutting or boosting the level of specific frequencies within a sound without effecting the rest of the sound.

Expander: The opposite function to that of a compressor, raising any signal below a user-defined threshold by a user-defined ratio.

Flanger/phaser: Forms of modulation, similar to chorus, but the original and delayed signals are combined in different ways to create different audible effects.

FX: Short for 'effects': Processes applied to a signal to alter its sound quality in some way, or the devices used to do so.

Gain: The stage of a pre-amplifier that boosts the level of a signal at the beginning of the signal path. A term commonly applied to any volume boost in the signal path.

Gating: An extreme form of expansion in which signals below a user-defined threshold are cut.

General MIDI: An agreed standard to ensure compatibility between MIDI equipment manufacturers. The term is now often used just to refer to the agreed list of 128 voices in the GM soundset or to the agreed standard for a set of drum/percussion sounds contained within MIDI compatible sound sources.

Harmony: The combination of chords used in a piece of music. To study harmony we look at the vertical aspects of the music (the chords, and how they change) instead of the horizontal aspects (the melody, and how it evolves).

Key: A term used to describe both the tonality of the music and the tonic note (the most important note in the tonal hierarchy).

Limiter: A compressor with an extremely high ratio setting.

Lo-fi: Low fidelity sound. A recording that is deliberately noisy.

Loop: A repeated passage. Often used to refer to samples that are imported into a sequence and repeated.

MIDI: Musical Instrument Digital Interface. An 8-bit computer language developed to allow electronic musical instruments to communicate with each other and the hardware necessary to facilitate this communication.

Mixing: The process of combining sounds. A master mix is the final result of the combination of all the component signals after they have been processed and combined.

Mono (Monophonic): A signal carried on one channel (in stereo systems the same signal would be heard on each channel).

Normalising: The process of boosting an audio signal so that the loudest point registers as 0dB.

Overdub: The process of adding additional tracks to previously recorded material.

Pan: The placing of a sound in the stereo field.

Plugin: A computer program written to either produce or manipulate audio within an existing audio sequencing package.

Resonance: The accentuation of a specific frequency – normally applied in context with the cutoff frequency in filters.

Reverb (Reverberation): The natural reflection of sounds from surfaces giving the impression of space. This is produced electronically by reverb units emulating aspects of natural reverb by mechanical/electronic means.

Sample/sampler: A sample is a short pre-recorded sound used in the context of a piece of music. Samplers are devices used to capture, edit, manipulate, store and playback samples.

Sequence/sequencer: A sequence is a piece of music input by means of a MIDI-capable device into a computer package which allows subsequent editing of almost every aspect of the MIDI data. A sequencer is the computer package used to facilitate the input and editing of MIDI data. Most sequencers are now capable of combining MIDI data and audio and are called audio sequencers.

Skeleton score: A musical score that has stripped back to several essential parts.

Signal-to-noise ratio: The level of wanted signal compared to the level of unwanted noise. A good signal-to-noise ratio is one in which the wanted signal is as loud as possible without clipping and the unwanted noise is inaudible.

Sound module: A hardware sound module is a standalone box that connects to a keyboard or computer by means of a cable (MIDI, USB, FireWire etc.) and needs to have its audio outputs connected to a mixing desk or headphones in order to hear the sounds produced.

Stereo (Stereophonic): A signal carried on two channels, left and right to represent a sound image as it might be picked up by two ears.

Syncopation: Placing strong beats where the pulse would normally dictate a weak beat, and/or weak beats where strong ones would be expected. Syncopation can occur on the beat, for example in reggae music where beats two and four (rather than one and three) are stressed; it can also occur off the beat.

Synthesiser: An instrument capable of producing sounds by combining different waveforms and/or pre-recorded, sampled voices. Synthesisers will normally have a piano-style keyboard and other methods of manipulating sounds during performance, but some need to be connected to an external keyboard in order to access the sounds they produce.

Tempo: How fast or slow music is played; the speed of the music. Indicated at the start of a piece by a word (such as 'fast' or 'moderate') or a metronome marking.

Texture: The sound quality of a piece, dependent on such features as the number of parts, the tone quality of the instruments and/or voices, and the spacing between the parts.

Timbre: The precise tone quality of a particular instrument, part or noise element in music. It may include a description of the speed of attack and decay of the sound, the nature of the elements that make up the sound (such as particular waveforms) and subjective opinions on the quality of tone.

Tonality: The use of major and minor keys in music and the ways in which these keys are related. Not all music is tonal – some is modal (based on one or more modes) and some makes use of non-western scales. Western pieces that use neither keys nor modes are described as atonal ('without tonality').

Velocity: The second data byte of a MIDI note on and note off message (within the range 0–127), determining the loudness of the note. It may also determine other characteristics of the timbre of the sound depending on how the sound source reacts to velocity data.